SOURCEPOINT THERAPY

EXPLORING THE BLUEPRINT OF HEALTH

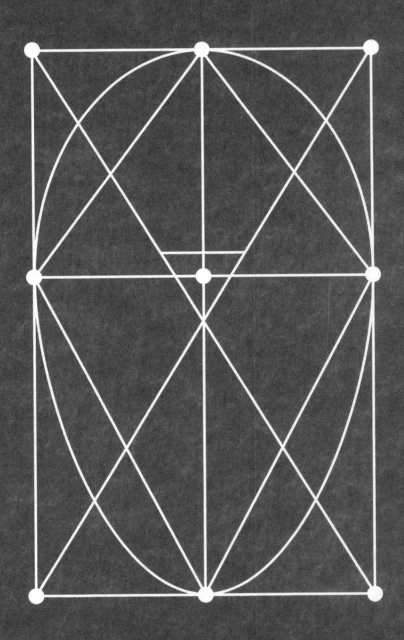

SOURCEPOINT THERAPY

EXPLORING THE BLUEPRINT OF HEALTH

By Donna Thomson
With Bob Schrei

MERLINWOOD BOOKS · EAST BLOOMFIELD, NY

The quotes referenced in this book are in no way intended to imply a personal endorsement of SourcePoint Therapy® or the contents of this book by the original author or speaker. Rather, in our own research and study we have found in the work of others many concepts and ideas that seem to us to resonate with the principles SourcePoint is founded upon. The references are intended to give readers the opportunity to continue their explorations with further reading, to expand their knowledge and inquiry, and arrive at their own conclusions.

This book is designed and illustrated by Richard Wehrman in partnership with Bob Schrei. Bob has been inspired in his teaching by the blackboard drawings of Rudolf Steiner and throughout the book you will find some samples of Bob's blackboard sketches from SourcePoint workshops.

Cover design by Richard Wehrman

Published by Merlinwood Books

+

THIS BOOK IS dedicated to you, the reader. You are the only reason this book was written. May it expand your consciousness and support your health, happiness and spiritual growth.

HER LOOM OF LIGHT

Born from light
into light
You return again to know yourself as light.
You are born from a precise order
a delicate balance
an eternal harmony
from the flow of the river
the cresting of the tide.
Born from the Mother of Mothers
the matrix
that nourishes and sustains, holds and protects.
You
are an exquisite expression of
Order, Balance, Harmony and Flow.
The perfection of all creation is yours.

You are woven into the shimmering fabric
of the starry night
the green of earth, blue of water
gold of sun, silver of moon.
A weaving of light and dark
skin and bone, heart and soul
an infinite vibration
a mandala of one arm span.
Light is the loom, love is the thread.
You are woven with love
a care and attention beyond imagining
from Her loom of light
that becomes
the body.

Do you know what that body is?
Look in the mirror of yourself.
The love you long for
the truth you seek —
You will find it in the whisper of your breath
the rhythm of your heart
the flow of your blood
the dance of your cells.
See your self as the pure and intricate reflection
of the cosmic Order
and love that self
with all your heart.

—Donna Thomson

TABLE OF CONTENTS

What is the Blueprint of Health?
An Overview of the Blueprint throughout Human History
The SourcePoint Perspective on the Blueprint
Order, Balance, Harmony, Flow: A Breath Meditation

The Diamond Points
The Golden Rectangle Points
The Navel Point and Sacral Point
Connecting to the Blueprint: A Diamond Point Meditation

The Mandala of the Body: Energetic Structures and Patterns
Geometry as the Language of the Blueprint
The Gold Point
The Golden Line and The Stick Figure
The Crescent Moon
The Eight-Pointed Star
The Golden Egg
Sacred Geometry: A Meditation

SourcePoint Therapy:
Exploring the Blueprint of Health

FOREWORD BY BOB SCHREI,
CO-FOUNDER OF SOURCEPOINT THERAPY®

Forewords, introductions, prefaces, prologues, a way in, a doorway;
all lead to what comes next. Enter here.

SOURCEPOINT THERAPY® provides a simple entry into the growing field √
of energy medicine, a means of accessing the Blueprint of health for the
human body. The Blueprint of health for the human body is the subject
of this book: what it is, how it expresses itself, how we can connect with
it. The Blueprint provides the foundation and the context for SourcePoint
Therapy.

As a perspective on how our body heals, SourcePoint is not a radical
new view. It has its roots and resonances in many healing and spiritual
traditions, in ancient views of who we are as human beings and how we
come into being. The story of the Blueprint for the human body has actually
been with us for millennia. Chapter One gives a brief overview of its history.

Perhaps these forgotten visions are re-emerging and that is why my
path unfolded as it did. With a formal background in architecture, I spent
many hours in my younger years as an apprentice and draftsman processing
blueprints in ammonia-filled rooms. These blueprints contained the
detailed information required to bring structures into being; in time they
would become homes, banks, churches, bridges, universities, skyscrapers
and so on. They were literally blue, with white diagrams and notes; hence
the term, *blueprint*. I found the idea of the blueprints intriguing in the way
they told the story of a form before its manifestation into physical reality.
My interest in blueprints persisted and transformed into a fascination
with human form and function. I wondered, how does organic life come

into being? How do we acquire the form and content of who we are as individual beings? Does that too require some kind of blueprint? In time, as I became drawn to the healing arts, I began to ask another related question: what sustains life and health? This is a universal question that arises in many philosophic, healing, and spiritual traditions, as well as in the field of science and in my own individual inquiry.

After much research, study and contemplation, I arrived at the view that human life and health is founded on and guided by a Blueprint, an energetic template for the human being that contains the information necessary to give rise to life and sustain health.

The approach to well-being outlined here, which is based on this idea of a specific energetic Blueprint for human health, arose from my desire to become better and more efficient in the work that I do, and to understand more deeply the nature of health. It was not an abstract inquiry. From the beginning, as I began to understand the nature of this Blueprint and explored how to connect with it consciously, I used the practices that emerged on a regular basis with my clients in my private practice of Rolfing®. I found quickly that this allowed me to address more effectively the many issues my clients presented each day.

SourcePoint is, above all else, practical. My primary interest is in seeing clients walk out the door feeling more aligned, more vibrant, more at ease, more comfortable in their bodies, more *themselves*, than when they walked in. As one of my clients said yesterday, "I feel soooo much better!" That is very gratifying for us both. And it is the heart of this work.

I am a Certified Advanced Rolfer, in practice since 1986. I have studied many different forms of manual medicine, as well as shamanism, spiritual healing, and other approaches to health. Alternative, or complementary, therapy is a vast field, unfolding with new perspectives every day. SourcePoint is a single point in that panorama; a single point that unfolds into a very practical approach that in my experience produces tangible results in the structure and function of our bodies.

SourcePoint is meant to be simple, but simplicity has its own challenges. When, after a single session utilizing SourcePoint, I see someone stand up with structural changes that would usually occur only after many hours of manual therapy, or when an acupuncturist integrating SourcePoint finds that the pulses are balanced in a way that might normally require much more attention, there is a direct challenge to our belief systems regarding how change happens. Yet, I have had these experiences, as have others. Many times, we find ways to rationalize such events and dismiss them, rather than remaining open and making an altruistic decision to explore a perspective that can be of real help to friends, family, and clients. We invite you to that exploration in this book.

In SourcePoint, the word "therapy" does not refer to a method of treating disease or symptoms but rather to a specific method of energy work designed to support the innate health of the body and all of its systems. This is the essence of holism, the foundation of all alternative medicine. However, even in holistic approaches, we often find that one aspect of health is emphasized over another, whether it is the physical, psychological or spiritual. From the SourcePoint perspective, true holism is to be found in and through the Blueprint. That universal Blueprint of health contains the source code: the information of the full potential of the human being in our most complete and vibrant state of physical, emotional, mental and spiritual health. The fundamental intention of SourcePoint Therapy is to connect to the Blueprint of health and facilitate its work. In doing so, it provides an energetic container and context for other healing modalities, physical, psychological, or energetic. SourcePoint is not intended to be a stand-alone practice, but rather as a support to whatever else people are doing for their healing.

Every discipline has its definition of health and how it is measured. However, we are all really asking the same question: how do we restore order and balance to a system that is out of balance? SourcePoint is another perspective, another attempt to answer that question. It is my hope that practices such as those of SourcePoint Therapy can contribute to the alleviation of our modern healthcare crisis, not as replacements for modern medicine, but as much-needed simple adjuncts, accessible to those who seek to keep themselves in balance in a world that is out of balance.

This book does not contain testimonials, stories of miracles, or accounts of individual healing journeys. We have stories, but we chose not to include them here. In part, this is because in SourcePoint Therapy the emphasis is not on the story. At the same time I have a deep respect for the privacy of my clients. It is my personal belief that people's stories have a powerful energy and their continued journey towards health is best served by keeping that energy contained within the boundaries of their personal lives.

In addition, each person's story is unique and unrepeatable. No one's journey will be like anyone else's. This is perhaps a dilemma in the practice of energy medicine in the modern world. Energy work is not predictable. There are no formulas. Each person is an individual requiring our full attention and knowledge. Every condition has multiple causative factors. That is why in SourcePoint Therapy we relate to the uniqueness of the individual, not to the condition or illness they present. What works for one person may not work for another.

There are no guarantees in the field of energy medicine, but what I can say is that all of the practices of SourcePoint were tested in my personal private practice for ten years before I began to teach it. Teaching and my work with people are inseparable for me. My private practice is where I see the results, expand my understanding, and never stop refining SourcePoint.

Many people have said, "SourcePoint Therapy has changed my life." Did it? We cannot claim credit for what occurs. The Blueprint of health is always working to nourish, repair and sustain us. Through SourcePoint, we help this process along, as do many other modalities. I accept the experiences of these people with humility and wonder, and hope that this method will continue to bring sustenance and support to others.

In this book, we invite you to explore the Blueprint of health for the human being with us. We give you some simple meditative practices for staying connected to the Blueprint, and these can be very helpful if practiced regularly. If you find you have an affinity with the principles and practices, we invite you to seek out a practitioner who utilizes SourcePoint and/or join us for SourcePoint training. We recognize that people have many demands on their time and resources so our workshops are intentionally small and affordable. We are committed to providing individual attention to all in a supportive environment. The trainings are short and this book itself is brief and simple.

As you will see, SourcePoint Therapy is based on some very profound principles; however, the practices are not complicated to learn and use. No prior background in the healing arts is required to attend a workshop, but practitioners of many modalities have found that SourcePoint adds an invaluable resource to their work. Often after a workshop, people will say to me these exact words: "This is the missing piece I've been looking for."

The full story of how this work came into being is told in greater depth at the end of the book. Between here and there, may what you read awaken a deep knowing within you of this primordial approach to your own health and well-being. May our collective awareness of the universal Blueprint of health, and our actualization of it, bring greater peace and harmony into the world, even as it supports the full potential of each individual.

Bob Schrei
Santa Fe, New Mexico
February 10. 2015

IN A COMPLEX WORLD, SIMPLICITY
HAS GREAT POWER.

SOURCEPOINT THERAPY® IS a simple approach to energy work for the 21st century and beyond. In this book we will explore the fundamental principles of SourcePoint. Everything we offer here is only a perspective based on our own experience, understanding and study. It is but one possible way of comprehending the mystery of healing, energy and consciousness, one way to explore our own essential nature and that of the universe that is our home. There are many perspectives available to us these days, and each person has to decide individually what resonates, what calls, what rings true, what helps.

This book is intended as an introduction for people who are interested in exploring the field of energy work for their own benefit, and for practitioners of other modalities who would like to enhance their existing practices with simple energy work methods and principles. Here are the basic premises upon which SourcePoint Therapy is founded and which we will be examining in this book:

1. There is a universal energy field in which we dwell, and that we are a part of. We call this universal energy simply Source. This universal energy field contains the information of Order, Balance, Harmony and Flow necessary to create and sustain all life.

2. Within this universal energy field are found blueprints for all forms of life. In SourcePoint Therapy our intention is to provide a means of connecting specifically with the Blueprint of health for the human being. This energetic template contains the information necessary to sustain physical, emotional, mental and spiritual health, including that of the highest potential we have as human beings.

3. We can access this Blueprint for the benefit of others and ourselves. The body has an inherent capacity to "download" this information of health. However, the connection to the Blueprint is often disrupted and weakened by many factors, such as accumulated stresses of daily life.

4. The purpose of SourcePoint Therapy is to help strengthen our connection to the universal Blueprint of health for the human being. Connecting to the Blueprint of health supports our health by re-attuning us to the flow of information from the Blueprint. With SourcePoint methods, we can also address energetic blockages that may be obstructing that flow.

5. SourcePoint Therapy provides an energetic container and context for whatever other modalities we use to help others or ourselves. It is intended to support, not replace, healing work that is done at the physical or psychological level and is not intended to be a stand-alone modality of therapeutic work.

We find the compelling presence of the Blueprint in ancient healing and philosophic traditions as well as at the frontiers of contemporary science. In this book you will learn about points in the human energy field that connect the individual physical body to the Blueprint, bringing that information to the body. In SourcePoint Therapy we also work with energetic structures and points on the body that strengthen and organize the individual energy field.

Since 1995 my husband, Bob Schrei, and I have been accessing the information that forms the ground of this work, exploring its fundamental principles, testing and refining the practices, and, in the early years of the 21st century, beginning to share it with others. People often ask us, "How did it begin?" "Where does this come from?"

There is a story of SourcePoint that is intimately tied to Bob's and my personal spiritual journey during this lifetime. We'll tell you that story, but not until the end of the book. That's because the work is not about us, and we have no particular agenda with it other than to share it as best we can for the benefit of others. For now, it's enough to know that the practices of SourcePoint emerged from the energy-information field of the Blueprint itself. We'd like you to explore that field with us now, to understand it, to feel how the information in this book resonates for you. It's your journey, just as it has been ours, to discover this energy field, become familiar with it, and learn to work with it as you choose.

You will have your own unique experience of the Blueprint once you pass through the open door that is waiting for you. This isn't a textbook. We can't teach you how to do SourcePoint Therapy in a book, any more than a dancer can learn how to dance by reading about it. You would need to attend a SourcePoint Therapy training to learn how to fully practice this system of energy work. However, what we can do in this book is introduce you to the essential principles and practices, and give you some meditative exercises for connecting to the Blueprint of health. Just exploring the principle of the Blueprint and becoming aware of its possibilities can help to shift one's view, moving the focus from ill-health to health.

Healing is not only a science; it is an art. This book is about the art of healing, its grace and beauty, how it comes to us unexpectedly, from the depths of our souls, from our connection to the Source of our being. The information of health, of Order, Balance, Harmony and Flow, is inherent in the universal energy; it is the essence of your personal life force energy. It is present in nature all around you, it radiates from the stars, the moon and sun. Health is our birthright, our fundamental nature. As soon as we begin to focus on the health inherent in our own bodies and in nature, our context for everything shifts.

Modern healthcare tends to focus on illness and disorder and prescribing specific physical treatments for them. That is also necessary, of course! It is important to directly address our pain and symptoms; there are appropriate medical modalities for doing that and we expect people to engage in those. But when we come from a foundation of remembering our essential health, when we recognize and call upon our innate resources, our healing journey takes on new and different dimensions. And the Blueprint for health is a powerful resource.

May the information in this book nurture your spirit and open the doors to love, joy, peace, abundance and health in your life. You, just as you are in this moment, are an exquisite expression of the universal energy. You are an integral component of it, a crucial point in a vast network. May this book help you to experience your essential wholeness and innate well-being.

CHAPTER ONE

The Blueprint

*'There is no use trying,' said Alice; 'one can't believe impossible things.'
'I dare say you haven't had much practice,' said the Queen. 'When I
was your age, I always did it for a half hour a day. Why, sometimes,
I've believed as many as six impossible things before breakfast.'*

—Lewis Carroll, *Alice in Wonderland*

THE IMAGINATION IS a powerful resource for healing and for understanding the nature of this universe that is our home. Too often the power to imagine is dismissed and discounted. "It's just your imagination" is one of the most common things an adult says to a child. It's also one of the most common things people say to themselves as they open up to the presence of greater consciousness, spirit and energy in their lives. So, at the very beginning of our exploration together, I want to encourage you to honor your imagination. Use it. Open yourself to a world you will never understand with your ordinary mind. We live in a universe so wondrous, so full of light, so magical and beautiful, that we need our imaginations to begin to comprehend it. A well-known quote from Albert Einstein emphasizes this: "Imagination is more important than knowledge. For knowledge is limited to all we now know and understand, while imagination embraces the entire world, and all there ever will be to know and understand." [1]

Imagine this possibility: you dwell within a matrix of energy filled with information of all kinds. What you perceive as empty space around you is not empty at all; it is actually filled with energy. And that energy is imprinted with information! You are surrounded by this field, and as intimately connected to it as a baby in the womb is to its mother. There is constant communication going on; messages are given and received.

Beyond our conscious awareness, we are constantly taking in, processing and transmitting information, and so is everything else. *We have a natural capacity to access the information present in the universal energy field.*

With that statement, the story of the Blueprint begins. Storytellers, priests, priestesses, shamans and scientists have been telling stories about the nature of our universe since humans first gathered around fires. Those stories are based on experience, observation and belief. Think how the science story has changed since the apple fell on Newton's head. Who knows how the story will read in another fifty or one hundred years?

Author and researcher Lynne McTaggart speaks of energy and information in her book *The Field: The Quest for the Secret Force of the Universe*: "There is no 'me' and 'not-me' duality to our bodies in relation to the universe, but one underlying energy field. This field is responsible for our mind's highest functions, the information source guiding the growth of our bodies. It is our heart, our brain, our memory—indeed, a blueprint of the world for all time. The field is the force, rather than germs or genes, that finally determines whether we are healthy or ill, the force which must be tapped in order to heal." [2]

The energy field described here is the world beyond the physical-material; it is the non-material realm from which form arises—Source. Let yourself imagine the possibility that this universal energy field contains energetic templates that are blueprints for everything: all life, the planets, the world, you and me. And in SourcePoint Therapy we are connecting with the specific Blueprint of health for the human being.

Take a moment more to get a sense of what we're talking about here, not with your intellect at this point but with your intuition. Imagine you are outside at night looking at a glorious star-filled sky. Become aware of the dark field in which those stars are shining—all that empty space in between. You remember what you've read here. That space is not empty at all. It's filled with information, invisible to the eye, just as the communications that travel to your cell phone are invisible. This information is being broadcast from the universal energy field on different wavelengths. You are the antenna, the receiver. You can select any channel you wish, and now you are tuning yourself to the health channel—the one that is broadcasting the information your human body needs to maintain itself—the Blueprint channel. SourcePoint provides the means to tune into that channel and receive its transmission.

Here is another straightforward contemporary metaphor tc stimulate your imagination of this specific energy field called the Blueprnt. All the data necessary to the health of your laptop, tablet or desktop computer is stored somewhere these days in "the cloud." Have you ever seen the cloud? Do you know where it's located? And yet, if your laptop is like mine, you could say that much of the information fundamental to your life is stored there, and you trust that information to be there when you need it. So it is with the Blueprint. We can't show it to you, we can't tell you exactly where it's located, but the practices of SourcePoint give us the IP address of the Blueprint. [3]

The Blueprint is a specific energy field that exists within the larger matrix of Source. The dictionary definition of *matrix* is "a situation or surrounding substance within which something else originates. develops, or is contained." [4] The word comes from the same root as the word *mother*. Source is the matrix of universal energy that contains all possibility. Every-thing originates from, develops within, and is contained by Source. *The Blueprint is a specific ordering, organizing energy field within this universal energy field that contains the information that gives rise to the human body and maintains its health.* Many forms of energy work seek to access universal energy. In SourcePoint our intention is to provide a method to connect with this specific energy field that is the Blueprint of health for the human being.

And what is the nature of this specific energy field we call the Blue-print? It is difficult to put into words, but the words that best describe the essence of this Blueprint are these simple ones: Order, Balance, Harmony and Flow. We will be working with and exploring these words throughout this book. For now, just use your imagination again. You are sitting by a flowing stream on a quiet day, at sunrise, when everything is emerging into activity, waking up, becoming. You feel at peace with yourself and the world around you, and somewhere inside you arises a sense that the universe is not just a random, chaotic set of meaningless events; there is purpose here. Even though you can't put it into words, you can feel it, in this quiet, in this moment, in the flow of the stream and the sound of the birds and the rising of the sun. Order, Balance, Harmony, and Flow are all around you. You feel it. You don't have to have it explained it you. There is a glimmer of understanding: *Ah, I know what those words mean.* You feel them as your fundamental nature, the nature of all that is. We've all had those moments of conscious connection, in one form or another. In the process of working with the Blueprint, you will come to know these words, their energies and their healing qualities, intimately.

The concept of the Blueprint is not a new one; before SourcePoint Therapy there was the Blueprint! Here is an overview of the Blueprint as expressed in various philosophical and healing traditions, as well as in contemporary biology and physics. Please remember that in each one of these perspectives, there is a possible lifetime of exploration to undertake. Here we give you merely a glimpse!

Remembering that the Blueprint is a specific energy-*information* field, we turn first to what Candace Pert says about the science of information theory in her ground-breaking book *Molecules of Emotion,* "…If information exists outside of the confines of time and space, matter and energy, then it must belong to a very different realm from the concrete, tangible realm we think of as 'reality'…Information theory seems to be converging with Eastern philosophy to suggest that the mind, consciousness, consisting of information, exists first, prior to the physical realm, which is secondary, merely an out-picturing of consciousness." [5]

We find the concept of the Blueprint in the discourses of Plato concerning the *Idea*, the ideal form that precedes our reality of the material world. These Ideas are not dependent on human thought, but have their independent existence in the archetypal realm. "It [Plato's Idea] is a primordial image or formal essence that … is the very foundation of reality itself." [6] At the root of our western philosophical tradition, there is this concept of an energetic form, the Idea that underlies and manifests into physical form. What we call the Blueprint for human health could also be called the Platonic ideal of human health.

Carl Jung is known for his work with archetypes. An archetype can be defined as a pre-existent form present in the collective unconscious. [7]

Specific archetypes contain specific information. We could define the Blueprint as the archetype of the original human. Jung said, "...the pattern of God exists in every man...this pattern has at its disposal the greatest of all his energies for transformation and transfiguration of his natural being. Not only the meaning of his life but his renewal and his institutions depend on his conscious relationship with this pattern in his collective unconscious." [8]

The Adam Kadmon, in the Kabbalah, is variously described as the primordial human being, the Universal Man, the archetypal human, or the divine template of the human being. Similarly, from the SourcePoint perspective we can say the Blueprint is an energy template that gives birth to, sustains and repairs the human body.

In the tradition of Tibetan medicine, the Root Tantra is considered one of its sacred texts. This particular text, which is studied at the beginning of one's training in Tibetan medicine, presents a picture of the human being in its ideal form, a reference point of comparison for diagnosing illness that has interfered with this fundamental order and balance. The Root Tantra contains the information of the qualities of the human body in its original, balanced state—in other words, a blueprint of health. [9]

From the perspective of Five-Element Acupuncture we are told: "Within us, everything operates according to a plan (or blueprint) for its function (digestion, respiration, circulation, menstruation, etc.). Nothing simply occurs randomly, but inevitably follows built-in natural laws. With a clear and sound plan in place, everything works in synch, harmoniously and smoothly. All parts 'know' what to do, when and where to do it, as well as what the contingency plans are, if the unforeseen arises." [10] There is a natural order to life that is a manifestation of the Blueprint.

Ida Rolf (the creator of Rolfing® Structural Integration) said: "A joyful radiance of health is attained only as the body conforms more nearly to its inherent pattern. This pattern, this form, this Platonic idea, is the blueprint for structure." [11]

Michael Kern, Doctor of Osteopathy, discusses this organizing field from the perspective of contemporary biodynamic cranial-sacral practitioners: "The Breath of Life [our vital life force energy] carries an essential blueprint for health, which Dr. James Jealous called the 'Original Matrix.' This blueprint is a deep and unwavering ordering principle." [12]

Morphogenesis is defined as the formation of the structure of an organism. Rupert Sheldrake, a contemporary biologist, has done extensive research exploring the morphogenesis of plants. He says, "Over the course of fifteen years of research on plant development, I came to the conclusion that for understanding the development of plants—their morphogenesis—genes, and gene products, were not enough. Morphogenesis also depends on organizing fields." [13] The Blueprint is an organizing field; it "informs" the manifestation of the physical body, shapes its development and supports its health. As we use our imagination as well as our intellect to reflect on this principle of the Blueprint, we begin to perceive the body more fully. We no longer see it as just a physical entity. It is, as Sheldrake says, "a nested hierarchy of vibrations within vibrations." [14] The physical body is actually crystallized energy fixated into certain form for a certain period of time.

In a recent article entitled "The Quantum Hologram and the Nature of Consciousness," Edgar Mitchell (also known as the sixth man to walk on the moon) and his co-author Robert Staretz, state: "We present a new model of information processing in nature called the Quantum Hologram ...It elevates the role of information in nature to the same status as that of matter and energy. We speculate that QH seems to be nature's built-in vast information storage and retrieval mechanism and one that has been used since the beginning of time. This would promote QH as a theory which is a basis for explaining how the whole of creation learns, self-corrects and evolves as a self-organizing, interconnected holistic system." [15]

Physicist F. David Peat speaks of abstract symmetries that underlie our everyday reality and that can be thought of as the archetypes of all material form. He references renowned physicist Werner Heisenberg in his discussion of this. "Heisenberg argued that ultimate reality is to be found not in electrons, mesons, and protons but in something that lies beyond them, in abstract symmetries that manifest themselves in the material world and could be taken as scientific descendants of Plato's ideal forms... these symmetries have an immanent and formative role that is responsible for the exterior forms of nature." [16]

Ervin Laszlo, well-known systems theorist, is the author of *Science and the Akashic Field: An Integral Theory of Everything*. In this book he synthesizes the research of contemporary physics and arrives at the conclusion that the quantum vacuum is the original energy and information field that informs the entire universe. Lazlo says: "The physical world is a reflection of energy vibrations from more subtle worlds that, in turn, are reflections of still more subtle energy fields. Creation, and all subsequent existence, is a progression downward and outward from the primordial source." [17]

In sum, what we are calling the Blueprint is a mysterious idea, form, concept, principle, and reality that appears and reappears over centuries of human thought and experience. As we complete our journey from the philosophers of ancient Greece to the work of contemporary scientists, we return to the concept of the Blueprint in SourcePoint Therapy.

We call this specific energy field that informs the human body the Blueprint because this is the word that most closely pinpoints the *function* of the information with which we are connecting. Just as the blueprint for a building gives the builder specific information regarding proportion, structure and design, so too the Blueprint we speak of in SourcePoint communicates the information needed to sustain health directly to the energy field of the individual human body. "Blueprint" implies something you can take hold of and work with. That is what SourcePoint is about: making the esoteric tangible, practical and accessible, bringing an awareness of this dimension of energy, vibration, pattern and information into people's everyday reality, for their benefit.

People often ask, "Is this my personal blueprint? Are you talking about DNA? Does my blueprint change?" From the SourcePoint perspective, our premise is that each person has his or her own individual energetic blueprint, with layers of ancestral, genetic and other influences interacting to produce the individual. In this view, DNA carries the information of the universal blueprint, as transformed by those other forces. DNA is not itself the Blueprint of health—it arises from it. The archetypal or universal Blueprint contains the information essential to all human beings. Our individualized blueprints are unique to each of us, according to ancestry, biology, genetics and many other influences, but all are grounded in that information of the universal Blueprint.

Our individual blueprint changes according to our experiences and influences, whereas the universal Blueprint is relatively fixed in nature. It is like the North Star that once guided sailors over the seas. They could count on it to be their reference point because it moved only slightly over a period of ten thousand years. Similarly, the information of the universal Blueprint, from the SourcePoint perspective, does respond over vast periods of time as human beings evolve and change. But the fundamental information of health for the human being remains steadfast, guiding us, sustaining our very existence.

It is the universal Blueprint we have been describing in this chapter, and that we connect to in SourcePoint. The universal Blueprint of health for the human being contains the fundamental information necessary for life, for optimal functioning. It is the precise information that makes us human, gives us form and brings us into manifestation. It contains the information for our highest potential as human beings. What is that highest potential? Open your imagination again in relation to this question. What is the highest potential of the human being? Do we, in our present consciousness, have any idea yet what human beings are capable of, in the positive sense of the word? How our innate capacities for creativity and compassion could manifest to change our lives and the world? How our imagination, intellect, intuition and understanding could continue to develop?

In Chapter 11 we will speak a bit of how, from the SourcePoint perspective, this human potential might manifest. But, really we don't know. None of us know, but many of us have a belief that there is much still to learn about being human, as yet unknown resources within us that can be tapped for the good of all. So when we say the universal Blueprint contains the information of the highest potential of the human being, we are saying that there is an intelligence inherent in the cosmic Order that knows more than we do about what we can become.

The universal Blueprint is what we all have in common. No matter our race, our genetics, our ancestry, our gender, our culture, there is the underlying pattern of the human, who we are at the core of our being, at our fullest potential. This is what we are working with. With SourcePoint we can access the Blueprint within ourselves, and we can access it in the universal energy field around us. There is no separation.

The principle of the Blueprint can seem abstract to people at first, but once you begin to work with it, to experience the effect of connecting with it, you realize it is a palpable reality as tangible as your breath, immediately accessible in a moment.

ORDER, BALANCE, HARMONY, FLOW: A BREATH MEDITATION

•

The breath is the key to connecting with the Blueprint on your own, for yourself, for now. As you focus on the rhythm of the breath, the in-breath and out-breath, just being aware of its natural rhythm, watching it slow itself down or speed itself up, you are entering a state of balance and harmony.

Sit quietly in the morning, or just for a moment in the midst of a busy day. Focus on your breath and feel its natural rhythm. Settle into the exhalation and the inhalation. Allow the words *Order, Balance, Harmony and Flow* to resonate with your breath, to permeate your consciousness. You will hear these words over and over throughout this book. We could call them the Source-Point mantra, the Blueprint mantra, an intonation that evokes the energy and qualities of the words themselves. Say them aloud, now, breathing in quietly and saying each word on the exhalation. As you experience the vibration and rhythm of these words, you immerse yourself in the Blueprint. You experience your own fundamental nature. *Order, Balance, Harmony, Flow.* That's what you are. That's your health, your life, your whole being, expressed succinctly and clearly by your own voice. Who am I? *Order, Balance, Harmony and Flow.* Address yourself by your true names, and you will begin to remember who you really are. Repeat the mantra of the Blueprint, and it will begin its work of transformation, bringing you into alignment with the fundamental Order, Balance, Harmony and Flow of the universal energy and the specific information of the Blueprint for the health of the human body.

When you are ready, bring your meditation to a close. In SourcePoint, we like to dedicate our work for the benefit of all beings everywhere. In workshops we end each meditation with the traditional phrase: *May all beings be happy, peaceful and free of suffering.* This provides closure and a transition into your daily life. It reminds you of the universality of the Blueprint.

•

The more you explore the principle of the Blueprint, the more you discover your connection to all that is. This can bring you delight and wonder; it can help you experience greater peace in the present moment. You begin to understand your place in the universe. Your mind opens. Perhaps you begin to think differently, and to understand healing in a new way. Your heart opens, allowing love to manifest. Your body opens, and energy flows more freely. You begin to understand the Blueprint not only with your rational mind, but also with your heart; your innate wisdom recognizes it. These experiences can begin to come to us as we open up to our full potential as human beings, in a single moment of our breath.

Audio versions of the meditations in this book are available on our blog, which can be found on our website:
www.sourcepointtherapy.com

CHAPTER TWO

Connecting to the Blueprint

...If we see deeply, everything is linked to everything else in the whole universe, and from one particle we can see the whole universe, which is included in it and out of which it is created.

—Thich Nhat Hanh, *The Sun My Heart*

MODERN PHYSICS AS well as ancient wisdom traditions tell us that self and cosmos are not separate, but are rather interdependent aspects of a larger Whole. Physicists describe an interactive and entangled universe in which subatomic particles, once they have made contact with each other, are then forever connected, and can communicate with each other, even over vast distances, instantaneously. This communication is non-local and not limited by the speed of light. This universe in which we dwell is a vibrant, sentient network that is constantly communicating with itself.

The Buddha is reported to have said: *in this fathom-high body is the arising and ceasing of the entire universe.* The microcosm reflects the macrocosm. We can know and understand the infinite by looking within. We can see the universe in the mirror of the self. For example, the human brain contains billions of neurons, all in intimate communication with each other, giving rise to complex neural pathways. The welcome receptors on these neurons receive information, create instantly up to 50,000 connections with other neurons, and pass the messages along. Our brains are wired for communication, just like the universe.

Furthermore, scientists have discovered that the brain contains detailed maps of every part of the body, including an area that extends approximately arm's length out from the body in every direction. In other words, the brain maps the physical body and also its immediate energy field, that is, the space around it. This could help explain the effect of off-the-body energy work.[18] Perhaps, if you touch a point in that space, the brain reacts to it just as it does if you touch the body itself!

From this we can begin to see that the physical body and its surrounding energy field are not two; they are intimately connected in a network of energy that is sentient, responsive, and communicative. Modern science is beginning to rediscover what the ancient seers in India knew: the *nadis,* or energy channels of the body, both permeate and surround the body (Figure 1).

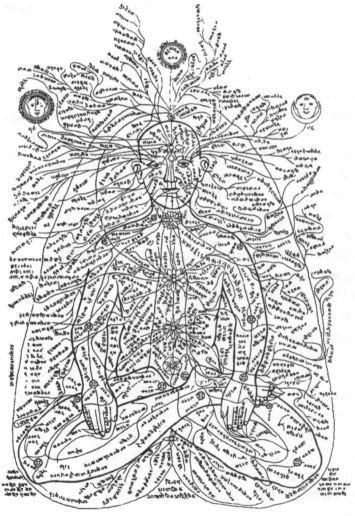

Figure 1

Take a moment now and use your imagination once again. Imagine your entire being in constant communication with the Blueprint of health present in the universal energy field, reflected in your very own body. Imagine the networks that compose the systems of your body. Feel the connections from brain to heart to belly, arms and legs, all the organs. Everything is communicating. That network extends out beyond the body into the immediate field around it, as scientists have discovered. Imagine that, and let your mind follow a network of pathways extending itself beyond the physical body into the immediate energy field, and then out into the far reaches of the galaxy. The channels are open, the lines are clear. You are communicating. You are connected. You are always linked to the universal Blueprint.

In SourcePoint we work from the perspective that the foundation of health is strengthened when the information of the Blueprint can flow freely to and in the physical body. We are always connected, but things happen to us that disturb, block or diminish that connection. SourcePoint helps us improve our communication with the healing energies inherent in the universal field. We work with specific points, located in the space around the physical body, whose function is to connect us to the Blueprint of health for the human being.

This is another fundamental principle of SourcePoint Therapy: *There are specific points in the energy field of the physical body that connect us to the specific energy template present in the universal energy field that is the Blueprint of health for the human being.*

Just as acupuncture points open the meridians of the body so that life energy can flow without obstruction, the points we work with open the gateway to the flow of information from the Blueprint. In SourcePoint we are working with meridians that extend beyond the individual energy field. We are connecting with the energy-information network that pervades the universal energy.

There are Ten Essential Points that are taught in Module One of SourcePoint Therapy: The Diamond Points, the Golden Rectangle Points, The Navel Point, and the Sacral Point. We will be continuing to explore the practice of the Diamond Points throughout this book. Only in SourcePoint trainings can we go more deeply into the use of the Golden Rectangle Points, the Navel Point, and the Sacral Point, but we can give a brief introduction here.

THE DIAMOND POINTS

Four fundamental points form the foundation of our practice and bring the information of Order, Balance, Harmony and Flow, inherent in the Blueprint, into the individual energy field of the physical body. These are the *Diamond Points*, so called because when held in sequence or visualized, they form a diamond shape around the body (Figure 2). Different traditions, including Tantra, the Kabbalah, and Taoism, make reference to the *diamond body*, which is described as the light body, the subtle body, or sometimes the energy double.

From the SourcePoint perspective, working with the diamond body—the energy field defined by these four points—opens a direct connection to the Blueprint and attunes the body to its frequency. As we hold these points for another, have them held for us, or visualize them for ourselves, we are making a strong and direct connection with the information of the Blueprint for the health of the human body and the full potential of the human being.

The first of the Diamond Points is located in the individual energy field, to the right of the body, at the level of the navel. The exact locations of these points can be seen in Figure 3 and will be described in the exercise at the end of the chapter. This first point is the *Source Point*, so called because it connects us directly into the Blueprint. Using the analogy of an electrical system, you could say that connecting with the Source Point is like plugging into the grid.

The second of the Diamond Points is the *Grounding Point*, located below the feet. Just as electrical connections have to be grounded, so does the energy-information of the Blueprint. To be grounded in the deepest sense of the word means to be rooted in our innate health, in the information of the Blueprint.

The Activation Point is the third of the Diamond Points. It is on the left side, directly across from the Source Point. This point activates the information of the Blueprint in the physical body, bringing us into alignment

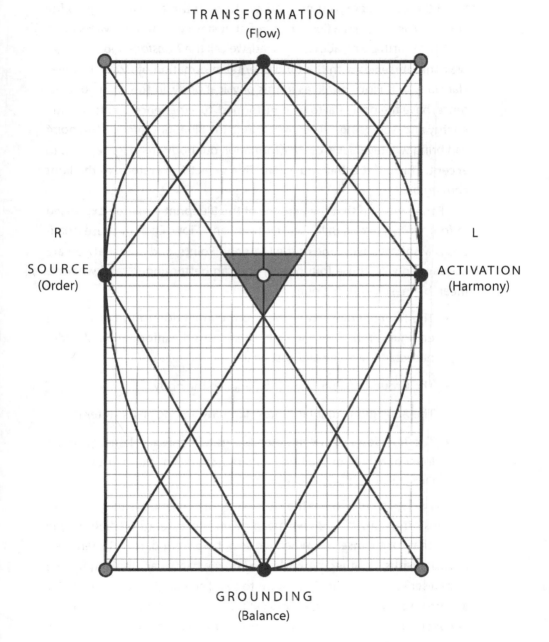

Figure 2

with it. To continue the electrical analogy, the Activation Point is the switch. Once the connection is grounded, we turn on the switch and get a full current. Then there is a flow of energy that stays with us and works in us.

The fourth point, above the head, we call the *Transformation Point*. As we align ourselves with the fundamental information of Order, Balance, Harmony and Flow, our lives in this physical body, in this plane of existence, have the potential to be transformed, to experience greater health, energy and well-being. The connection to the Blueprint through this point can bring whatever level of transformation our body-mind is prepared to accept. This point is the equivalent, in an electrical system, to the light coming on!

Earlier we said that the essence of the Blueprint could be expressed in four words: Order, Balance, Harmony and Flow. Each of these qualities is associated with one of the Diamond Points, and now that you are acquainted with those four points, you can better understand what we mean by these words in SourcePoint.

- The Source Point strengthens our connection to the organizing energies of the Blueprint, which contains the information of Order necessary to create and sustain life.

- The Grounding Point brings Balance to the body.

- The Activation Point facilitates Harmony among all its systems.

- The Transformation Point then brings a freer Flow of energy to the individual field of the body and its systems, in alignment with the Order inherent in the Blueprint.

As we open ourselves to the Blueprint we are opening to the possibility of transformation. What do we mean by transformation? We find people know that for themselves. When we seek help from different therapies, spiritual paths, or other methods, we know what we are looking for; we have a sense of the change we want to see. The practices of SourcePoint are there to support transformation in the direction of our greatest good, our deepest intentions, our highest potential, and our health at every level, spiritual, mental, emotional, and physical.

Transformation always means letting go of something. The Transformation Point helps us to let go of the painful, familiar patterns of the past. It opens us to the energy of the unknown. Often in the inner healing process we come to the threshold of transformation and stop, or we go back and forth. We get better, and then regress. We often find the process of transformation is an ongoing, non-linear process. It is not always immediate improvement. Energies will shift into a different pattern, but that different pattern will not always hold right away, and so it is supportive when we are in the midst of change to have a regular connection with the Blueprint, to continuously feed the body that information of Order, Balance, Harmony and Flow. Meditation and visualization with the Diamond Points can help to maintain the continuous flow of information, especially when supported by regular SourcePoint sessions and consistent attention to our physical well-being in the form of proper nutrition, exercise, and appropriate therapies and medicines.

The Diamond Points can guide you in your daily life in many situations. Remember the practice of connecting to the points, which you will learn at the end of the chapter. Use the framework of Order, Balance, Harmony and Flow to guide you. Ask yourself questions such as these: If you are tired: *What do I need to bring a greater Flow of energy?* If you are stressed: *What do I need to bring greater Balance?* In situations of conflict: *What will bring greater Harmony?* In any circumstance: *How can I bring Order, Balance, Harmony and Flow to the situation? How can I connect to my full potential? How can I be more grounded in this situation? What is blocking the activation of what I know to be true from manifesting in my life? How can I allow this situation to transform?*

Often it will seem as though the answers to all these questions are simply, *I don't know.* However, think of these as Zen-like koans, those spiritual questions that Zen masters pose to open their students' minds. You are not supposed to answer them literally, nor try to figure them out. As you inquire in this way, the questions themselves open a doorway into greater awareness of those organizing energies of Order, Balance, Harmony and Flow. The inquiry itself connects you to that field of the Blueprint.

Working with the Diamond Points is an expression of intention, which is important in healing work, as it is in every area of life. When we connect with these points through practice or meditation, we are expressing intention in a way beyond words. The points carry the intention of strengthening the connection to the Blueprint of health, to its natural Order, Balance, Harmony and Flow.

In Lynne McTaggart's book *The Intention Experiment,* she reports on a study in which a well-known healer was asked to form different intentions while holding five different Petri dishes in which cancer cells were growing. All the samples showed some reduction in cancer cell growth as a result of their being energetically infused with intention. However, the greatest reduction came with holding the simple intention that the *natural order* of cell growth be restored.[19] You have seen by now that connecting to that natural order is the foundation of all SourcePoint work. The fundamental intention of SourcePoint Therapy is to connect the person to the Blueprint and let the information of health, of Order, Balance, Harmony and Flow, do its work. As stated earlier, the points themselves carry the intention of connecting with the Blueprint. Every time you hold the points for another person or visualize them for yourself, you are entering into that intention and establishing the context of health.

THE GOLDEN RECTANGLE POINTS

The Diamond Points create an energetic container for the information and energy of the Blueprint to work. The second set of points, the *Golden Rectangle Points*, strengthen that container and further facilitate the work of the Blueprint in the body in a positive, balanced and specific way. These points are located in a rectangle around the body on a diagonal from the Sacrum (Figure 2). We will discuss the Golden Rectangle as an energetic structure in Chapter Three.

THE NAVEL POINT

The *Navel Point* is a microcosm of the individual being and functions as a gateway to bring universal life force energy to the body, which nourishes and sustains the individual energy. That energy has its own intelligence. It knows exactly where to go in the body and what frequency is needed to bring Order and Balance. The navel is our personal connection to the experience of wholeness, reminding us of our relationship to the cosmos, the heavens as we see them every night, the vastness of stars, space, and planets. The Navel Point links us directly with the moment of our manifestation into form, with conception, birth, and incarnation.

THE SACRAL POINT

The intention of the *Sacral Point* is to awaken and nourish the vital life force energy of the body. We will explore the sacrum further in Chapter Four.

People often ask us: How did you discover these points? We will go into this further in Chapter Twelve, but for now let's go back to the history of acupuncture for a parallel: "Acupuncture is rooted in the Taoist tradition, which goes back over 8000 years. The people of this time period would meditate and observe the flow of energy within and without."[20] This is exactly how the points of SourcePoint Therapy made themselves known. As we meditated and entered into a state of focused Awareness, seeking the information of Order, Balance, Harmony and Flow, the points revealed themselves. We observed them and worked with them, first with ourselves, and then with others. The process manifested as a spiral: working with the first points that emerged opened the doorway into further observations and more information, more points.

SourcePoint differs from acupuncture, however, in that the points we work with are not associated with specific conditions or illnesses of the body. We do not utilize the points to treat particular disorders or imbalances within bodily systems. Rather, the points—and patterns they form—work to connect to the information of health in the larger field and anchor that information in the individual energy field.

That information knows what to do. It has its own intelligence. If you are a health practitioner, bringing in this information will support whatever modality you are using. You do not use the points instead of your usual treatments. The Blueprint becomes the context of your work. If you are using the points for your own health, you do not neglect to get care at the physical level in whatever way you choose. While working with this energetic approach, you always attend to your health at the physical level as well.

Let's imagine again. Imagine the entire universe as a vast network of energy, manifesting as tiny golden seeds of light, dancing in ever-shifting patterns, like a net, a grid, a web. Imagine each point of light as a mirror. Everywhere on the net, light reflects light. You are a point of light woven into this net. What we call the self is a manifestation of light, each point uniquely itself and yet intimately related to every other point, reflecting every other point. In the eastern traditions, this image of the universe and the self is called *Indra's Net*. May it help you expand your mind and heart and vision to encompass the brightness that you are. As Lama Nyoshul Khenpo Jamyang Dorje says in *The Mirror of Essential Points*: "In this there is not a thing to be removed, nor anything that needs to be added. It is merely the immaculate, looking naturally at itself." [21]

When you connect to the Blueprint, it reflects back to you the image of your natural perfection.

CONNECTING TO THE BLUEPRINT:
A DIAMOND POINT MEDITATION

Stress is an ongoing factor of human existence. We may find ways to reduce the stress in our lives, but we can't escape it. From the SourcePoint perspective, stress disorganizes the individual energy field; it also weakens our connection to and alignment with the Blueprint. Remembering the principle of the Blueprint and doing some of the practices of SourcePoint Therapy regularly may help you to experience a greater calm, relaxation and ability to cope with the stress in your life. Currently there is much research being done on the beneficial effect of meditation on health, the brain, and how it reduces the effects of stress. Just do an Internet search on "meditation and health" or "meditation and the brain" and you will find plenty of fascinating references to explore.

The practices of SourcePoint Therapy are meditative in nature; however, you have something to do, you aren't just sitting there. For many people meditation becomes a frustrating and discouraging practice as they struggle to simply sit still and let go of thought. With this meditative practice of SourcePoint you are actively focused on a positive affirmation of health, while the points do their work and help you stay aligned with the Order, Balance, Harmony and Flow of the universal energy.

Before we describe the practice itself, please take time to familiarize yourself with the location of the points in relation to the body. Each point is located in the field of the body, twelve to eighteen inches out from the body, at the level of the navel (Figure 3).

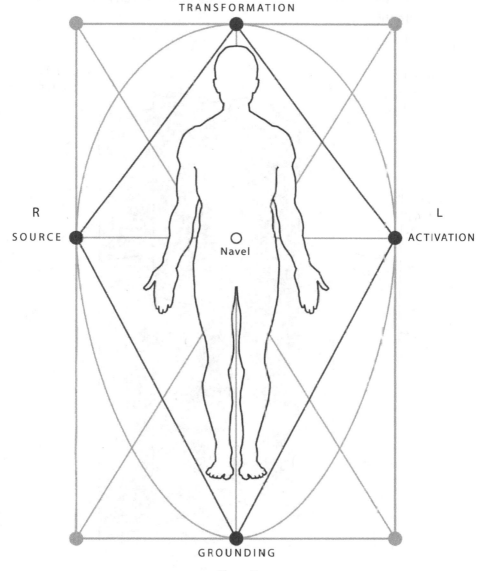

Figure 3

These points are located along the Coronal Plane of the body, which divides the body into anterior and posterior portions (Figure 4).

When doing the practice, lying down is the best position to begin with; later you can easily do it standing or sitting.

Also, don't be intimidated by the word visualize. What it really means is to *sense* the points around you in whatever way works best for you: you can see them in your mind, you can feel them, or you can just tell yourself they are there.

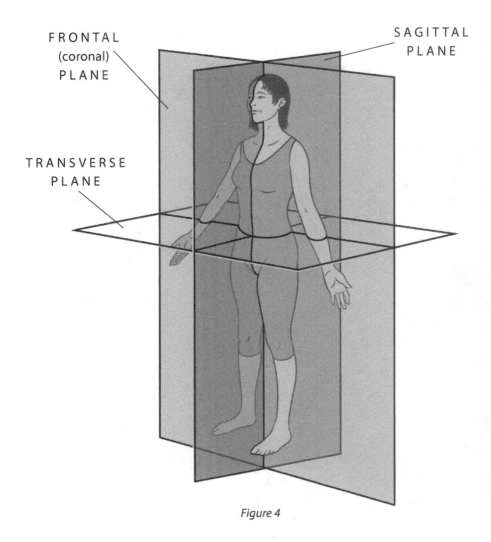

Figure 4

Now we are ready to begin the practice. Please read through the whole exercise before trying it. You will probably find it is most easily done with eyes closed.

•

In SourcePoint meditative practices, always begin with the Blueprint Breath Meditation found in Chapter One. Take a few minutes to attune yourself to that rhythm. Then, visualize the Diamond Points around you. You can hold them for yourself with your mind, just as a practitioner uses the hand to hold them for another person. This is very simple.

1. Begin with the Source Point. Remember, it is located out from the navel, twelve to eighteen inches from the body, on the Coronal Plane. Locate your navel by touching it with your hand and then move your attention twelve to eighteen inches out from the body on the right side. Imagine the point in some way. Feel it. Visualize it as a tiny golden seed point. Or, simply tell yourself: *I am observing a point to the right of my body that is my connection to the Blueprint of health.* Keep your attention there. Voice the word "*Source*" either silently or aloud.

2. Move your attention from the point on the right to the point below your feet. This is the Grounding Point, located also twelve to eighteen inches from the body. Stay there as long as you like. Bring the word "*Grounding*" to mind, or vocalize it.

3. Move your attention to the Activation Point, twelve to eighteen inches out from the body at the level of the navel, on the left side. It is directly across from the Source Point. Let your mind rest there. "*Activation.*"

4. Finally, move on to the Transformation Point, located twelve to eighteen inches above the head, opposite the Grounding Point. Feel that point above you and rest your mind there once again. Verbalize or think the word "*Transformation.*"

You can also repeat the words *Order, Balance, Harmony and Flow* as you do this. Remember, *Order* is associated with the Source

Point, *Balance* with the Grounding Point, *Harmony* with the Activation Point, and *Flow* with the Transformation Point.

Always begin with the Source Point on the right and move in sequence to the Transformation Point above the top of the head. Always do all four points.

Bring your attention to each point, but don't strain. Don't struggle to hold onto any point. What we mean by *holding the point* is letting the mind dwell there. If your attention wanders, simply return it to that point, becoming aware that you have wandered and you are returning. What matters is the return.

As you practice, you will notice sometimes that you will want to dwell on certain points for a longer period. That's fine. You will know when it is time to move on. Sometimes you will also find that only a few seconds may be required at a particular point. That's fine too.

If you like, you can visualize a tiny golden seed of light at each point. You can connect the points with a thin golden line to form the diamond pattern around you. This can help to strengthen the boundaries of your individual energy field.

After completing the sequence of the Diamond Points, rest quietly, bringing your attention back to the breath. Be aware of the *vertical-horizontal axis* formed by the Source-Activation Points and the Grounding-Transformation Points. *The energetic midline* of the body connects the Transformation Point to Grounding Point. You can trace this with your mind if you like. The midline formed by the Grounding-Transformation Points is a powerful and strengthening energetic structure, as is the diamond pattern around the body.

•

Make this meditation a part of your daily routine. You can spend a long time with it, but it can be done also in about thirty seconds. You can't say you don't have time! As you do this you commit to shifting your focus to the Blueprint of health over and over. In addition, people who have an already established meditation practice find it is helpful to begin with this meditation. The Diamond Points provide a transition from activity to stillness, and an energetic container for other meditation.

To stay connected to the Blueprint is a discipline, a practice and an intention, all together. It is a practice that can help bring greater Order, Balance, Harmony and Flow to your whole system.

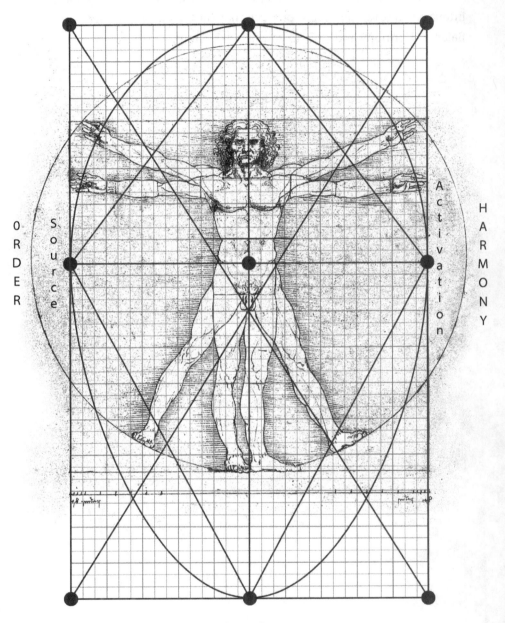

FLOW
Transformation

ORDER

Source

Activation

HARMONY

Grounding
BALANCE

Figure 5

CHAPTER THREE

The Inner Temple:
Strengthening the Energetic Structure of the Body

*It became increasingly clear to me that the mandala is the center. It is
the exponent of all paths. It is the path to the center, to individuation.*

—Carl Jung, *Memories, Dreams and Reflections.*

WHEN I WAS a child, I loved to connect the dots. I had books in which the
pages were covered with seemingly random black dots scattered over a
blank white surface. I could draw lines between the points, connecting
one to another and then another. A meaningful, recognizable pattern
would emerge: a boy, a girl, a dog, a cat, a tree, a star. Then, even more
wonderfully, I could take my crayons and make these images any color I
wanted. When I was done, the page was filled with form, color, movement
and meaning.

In this chapter we are going to connect the dots and examine the
mandala of the human body. From the SourcePoint perspective, a mandala
can be described as a geometric pattern that reflects the cosmic order. The
physical body has its own mandala, comprised of the energetic patterns
and structures that support, permeate and contain it. We call this *the Inner
Temple*, the sacred core of our being. There are two aspects of the Inner
Temple, inter-related and inseparable. The physical aspect is the internal
structure of the body, with its chambers, structures, skeleton, organs,
systems, and processes. However, the Inner Temple is also the Blueprint
made manifest in individual form, the exquisite and precise structure of
light and energy that supports the body from within.

In Figure 2 you have had a glimpse of this mandala from the Source-Point perspective. Together, the Diamond Points, the Golden Rectangle Points, the Navel Point, and the Sacral Point form this essential energetic structure of the Inner Temple of the human body while transmitting the energy and information of the Blueprint. If you connect the dots (i.e. these points) you can see the geometric patterns they form. Here we have another fundamental principle of SourcePoint: *Geometry is a primary language of the Blueprint, a medium through which it communicates the essential order of existence.*

Michael Schneider says in his book *A Beginners Guide To Constructing the Universe*: "Nature itself rests on an internal foundation of archetypal principles symbolized by numbers, shapes, and their arithmetic and geometric relationships... Modern scientists are reaffirming what the ancients observed in their world and taught in their myths: that a consistent language of geometric design underpins every level of the universe, from atoms through galaxies." [22]

Modern scientists are indeed reaffirming this principle of underlying geometric design. In 2010 an article appeared in *Scientific American* entitled "The Geometric Theory of Everything." In this article the authors, physicists A. Garret Lisi and James Owen Weatherall, state: "In fact, physicists think that everything in the world—all the forces of nature and even all the particles of matter—arises from different kinds of fields. The behavior of these fields hints at an underlying geometric structure." [23] In other words, "Deep down, the particles and forces of the universe are an expression of exquisite geometry." [24]

Leonardo Da Vinci's *Vitruvian Man* (Figure 5) vividly demonstrates the inherent geometry of the body. This drawing is one of the most reproduced graphic images ever. It reveals the proportions and patterns of the physical relationships within the body and also delineates its energetic structure. When you look at the human body from this perspective, you don't just see skin, bones, organs, arteries, and nerves. You see triangles, spheres, squares, rectangles, stars, lines and points. You see the Divine Proportion and the Golden Line. As sacred geometry expert Robert Lawlor says, you see "the architecture of bodily existence." [25]

From the point emerges the line, from the line pattern arises, and from pattern ever more complex structures manifest. There is an underlying geometry of the body that contains and expresses the information of Order, Balance, Harmony and Flow. There are also specific energetic/geometric structures, from the SourcePoint perspective, which provide a container and framework for the unimpeded flow of life energy within the body.

The pattern that appears when the *Diamond Points* are connected attunes the body to the frequency of the Blueprint. It outlines the energetic boundary of the individual energy field. Working with the Diamond Points can help you define and maintain your boundaries in interactions with others.

The Golden Rectangle formed the foundation for the temples of ancient Greece and was used in the construction of cathedrals in medieval Europe. The architects of those times knew instinctively that the proportions of the Golden Rectangle provided a container for the spiritual in the material dimension. They understood the wisdom of reflecting the cosmic order in the physical structure. In relation to our bodies, the Golden Rectangle is a fundamental energetic structure that contains and protects the Inner Temple of the body. It houses the essence, the Diamond Body, here on this plane of existence (Figure 2). People often speak of the soul dwelling in the body, but it can also be said the body dwells in the soul; that it is the physical manifestation of the soul. The configuration of the rectangle is the container on the physical plane for our spiritual essence. The pattern formed by the Golden Rectangle Points grounds us in our connection to the soul, and helps us to live in the world from that foundation. It stabilizes, harmonizes, and helps us to define boundaries.

The Golden Rectangle as an energetic structure in the energy field assists with the process of embodiment. Often in bodywork, movement work and in many self-help books, we are instructed to be more fully in our bodies. What we need, in order to follow this instruction effectively, is to understand what this body is, what it is we should inhabit more completely. No one thinks of the body as something requiring definition. In SourcePoint, when we refer to the body, we do not make a distinction between what is called the energy body and the physical body. *We are looking at the* body as an energetic structure. The physical form is a manifestation of energetic structure, and it is not separate from energetic structure. Physicality is energy and what is commonly called the energy body is a subtle form of physicality. The Golden Rectangle helps us experience this unified state.

The Navel Point is the focal point of the Inner Temple. In the Hindu tradition, the *bindu* is considered to be the single point, the seed point, from which the entire universe emerges. We can say the Navel Point is the seed point of each individual's unique pattern. Focusing on this point is energizing, nourishing, and sustains the flow of the vital life force energy within the individual. While activating this point is very simple, it works at profound and subtle levels of energy. That's why we don't go into more detail here regarding how to work with it. We study and practice this point—in depth—throughout SourcePoint Therapy training.

The Sacral Point—indeed the sacrum itself—constitutes an important aspect of the Inner Temple that we will examine in Chapter Four.

These points form a powerful geometric mandala through which you can connect to the Blueprint and access the information of Order, Balance, Harmony and Flow. Based on all we have been discussing, we can formulate another fundamental principle of SourcePoint: *In SourcePoint Therapy we work to repair and strengthen the energetic structure and boundaries of the individual being to provide a balanced, harmonious container for the flow of the universal energy in the body.*

In the course of life experiences, especially ones that are traumatic and stressful, those energetic boundaries and structures tend to get compromised. Maintaining the clarity, coherence and strength of our energetic boundaries and structures is as essential to health as a free flow of energy. Many energy therapies work with the flow of energy; in SourcePoint we work to maintain a healthy balance of flow and structure in the body and all of its systems.

Take a moment to reflect on the balance of fixation and flow in your life. Do the structures of your life provide a balanced container for the healthy flow of energy, or do they restrict it? How much of that restriction actually comes from your attitude toward those structures? Is there insufficient structure, resulting in an erratic and unbalanced flow of energy?

Where do you need to make changes to bring flow and structure into greater balance? To experience Source, your universal nature that knows no boundaries, and to simultaneously understand yourself as an individual with strong energetic boundaries, brings spiritual balance and physical health. Too often we get caught up in one extreme or the other. We insist on our individuality and dwell in the ego, and our boundaries solidify into rigid and defensive armor. Or we merge into that universal energy and refuse to recognize the challenges and gifts of working with material form, boundary and body. We end up not taking good care of ourselves. When we begin to understand the multi-dimensional nature of self and universe, we can find the appropriate balance. As we understand the importance of pattern and structure in maintaining our health we experience greater Order, Balance, Harmony and Flow in our lives.

Exploring the Inner Temple, we begin to understand the true meaning of the term *healing arts*. In a universe of harmonious pattern, we work with pattern to bring harmony into the individual energy field. With the points, we simply connect to the Blueprint and let its information do the work. However, the energetic patterns/structures of SourcePoint Therapy have specific functions in terms of strengthening, stabilizing, supporting and nourishing our energy as well as grounding the physical body in its connection to the Blueprint. We can trace certain patterns directly into the field, thereby strengthening the energetic structure of the body. In working with these we not only access the information of the Blueprint, we use pattern and structure directly to re-align and reorganize the energy field, to bring the information of Order, Balance, Harmony and Flow to the field. Working with the energetic structures of the body, an energy work practitioner becomes artist and architect, restoring the natural harmony of the body's original mandala.

Many cultures have their healing mandalas. We find one example of this in the Navajo tradition where the healer creates a sand painting using different colored sands, incorporating specific designs and images. "The mandala is primarily an *imago mundi*; it represents the cosmos in miniature . . . Made symbolically contemporary with the Creation of the

World, the patient is immersed in the fullness of life; he is penetrated by the gigantic forces that . . . made creation possible." [26]

To paraphrase this quote, the mandala not only represents the forces of creation at work, at an energetic level, it contains and transmits the information and energy of those generative ordering forces. In traditional ceremonies, the mandala is literally drawn around the body. Outside observers may miss this fundamental aspect of the ritual: *the mandala is not an abstract concept. The mandala is an actual reflection of those ordering forces manifesting in the physical realm*, organizing themselves into form and structure and being. To connect directly with those ordering forces brings energy, and—to use these words yet again—Order, Balance, Harmony and Flow into one's whole being. This is the foundation of many shamanic ceremonies. In SourcePoint we are working with these creative energies and energetic patterns and structures in a different way, a way that is not bound to any one cultural form, but uses the universal language of geometry to communicate with the body.

Like the mandalas used in time-honored healing ceremonies, the structures and patterns we utilize in SourcePoint are not symbols, as we tend to think of symbols, metaphors or representations. The energy patterns that we work with, which manifest the information of the Blueprint into this dimension, are living realities that underlie and permeate our visible reality. In modern life these archetypal forces have lost their charge. With SourcePoint Therapy we recharge the connection to what is now thought of as symbolic or mythological, to realms of experience and information and energy that are every bit as alive and active and powerful as our everyday reality.

The patterns and energy structures we work with are the Gold Point, the Golden Line, The Stick Figure, the Crescent Moon, the Eight-Pointed Star and the Golden Egg. These are taught in SourcePoint Therapy Module Two; however, we can describe them briefly here, as some of them may be used in meditation.

THE GOLD POINT

●

In SourcePoint we work with the Gold Point as another method of accessing the Blueprint, a connection to the cosmic energy of Order, Balance, Harmony and Flow. The Gold Point is the seed that contains the information of the whole, of the Blueprint. It radiates energy that supports the order and flow of the energy systems of the body. In your meditation practice with the Diamond Points, you have already learned how to work with the Gold Point. This tiny energetic structure has many appl cations in SourcePoint Therapy; for example, we utilize it in our work with chakras, as covered in Module Two of SourcePoint training.

A few words about the use of golden light in SourcePoint: the ancient alchemists spoke of the literal and spiritual transformation of lead into gold. When we work with energy we seek to transmute the "lead" of our old patterns into the "gold" of our full potential. When we visualize the points and structures in SourcePoint, we work with golden light. Often people will see different colors when working with the points. However, no matter what we see, we work with gold: the Golden Rectangle Points, Gold Point, the Golden Line, the Golden Egg. This connects us to Source, providing a ground, a connection to a universal frequency. We leave it to the Blueprint to decide what frequency, what color of light, may be needed in each particular situation. The colors we sometimes see are simply what the Blueprint is bringing, the universal light manifesting into this world of form.

Golden light reminds us of the light of the sun. It enhances and nourishes the life force. Think of it metaphorically, remembering the imagination is a useful avenue to understanding the world of energy. The sun awakens the life inherent in the seed planted deep in the earth. The seed grows toward the light. In working with golden light we awaken our potential for transformation, the seed in us that is oriented to the light, to the information of health which causes us to grow in a balanced way, and equilibrates us when we are out of balance.

THE GOLDEN LINE AND THE STICK FIGURE

From the Gold Point emerges the Golden Line, the energetic midline of the body that extends from the Transformation Point to the Grounding Point. This line is essential to the coherence of the internal energetic structure of the body. It passes through the body, on the coronal plane of the body, in front of the spine. It is the body's *axis mundi,* the energetic core around which the body and its energies organize and manifest.

From that line emerges the Stick Figure, another important organizing energetic structure. The Stick Figure is exactly what it says. You've seen a child's drawing of the human body. That's the Stick Figure! We also see this simple delineation of the body manifested in the petroglyphs of ancient cave peoples. The Stick Figure pattern is the energetic inner armature of the body, a natural extension of the Golden Line, again providing a structure that supports and organizes the individual field. Work with the midline and the Stick Figure strengthens the central channel of energy in the body's core.

The Golden Line and the Stick Figure are among SourcePoint's most effective tools for healing arts practitioners because they can help restore a steady, open flow of energy throughout the entire body. See Chapter Eight for more on the profound implications of these simple structures.

THE CRESCENT MOON

The crescent moon has long been a symbol of the Great Mother. Even today Our Lady of Guadalupe is still shown standing on the crescent moon.

In ancient times, the Great Goddess wore the crescent moon upon her head, stood upon it, held it in her hands, wielded it as blade and offered it as chalice. She was clothed in robes of stars and moons. The Great Mother is the matrix from which all life arises and to which all life returns. She is intimately connected with the rhythms of the tides and seasons, with ebb and flow—just as is the moon. In SourcePoint we find working with this energetic structure, the Crescent Moon, to be helpful in restoring the natural rhythms and tides of the body's energy. It can be calming, nourishing and strengthening.

THE EIGHT-POINTED STAR

From the earth, you can see the stars. The Star is a direct energetic connection between heaven and earth. It's a doorway, a portal and a bridge from one dimension to another. When you wish to journey in consciousness, to move from one frequency to another, the Star guides you and opens the gateway. In this material world, the pattern of the Eight-Pointed Star is the compass rose. It indicates the different directions and guides you to your destination. To work with this mandala strengthens your inner compass, grounds you firmly on the earth while opening you to higher dimensions, and helps you to orient yourself as you navigate this life, as you work with the body's energies, systems and structures.

In SourcePoint, we utilize the Eight-Pointed Star as a placeholder for the information of the Blueprint. Literally, it carries the information of the perfect Order, Balance, Harmony and Flow of the Blueprint as well as the universal radiant life force energy of Source. It is a powerful mandala for meditation. It's a good image to hold in the mind while you are doing energy work with clients, and in your own meditation.

We will work more with the Eight-Pointed Star in Chapter Seven .

THE GOLDEN EGG

If you connect the Diamond Points with a thin gold line in your meditation, they will form an actual diamond pattern or, if you arc the lines, they
will form an oval, a golden egg of light. (See also Figure 2.) This energetic
structure also contains the physical body and strengthens its energetic
boundaries. It is nourishing and energizing. We'll utilize this energetic
structure in meditation in Chapter Five.

For now, take a moment to experience the ordering energy of
geometric pattern directly. It isn't necessary to use these specific energetic
structures we have been discussing to do this. More familiar geometric
patterns such as triangles, rectangles, circles, squares, straight lines and
spirals all have the power to calm and soothe, balance and harmonize.
For millennia, philosophers, mathematicians, mages, healers and spiritual
seekers have explored the realm of Sacred Geometry and experienced the
transformative power of geometric pattern. Perhaps now, after reading
this chapter, you can understand better why it is called *Sacred Geometry*.
As we have seen, geometry is at the very root of our being, reflecting and
manifesting the natural order of the cosmos. It has profound implications
for healing and spiritual practice. Experiment, use your imagination, and
see how simple geometric structures can bring you into greater alignment
with the natural Order, Balance, Harmony and Flow of the universal energy.

SACRED GEOMETRY: A MEDITATION

•

After reading this, close your eyes and imagine in front of
you, in a field of white light, a golden square, a golden triangle and
a golden circle. If you visualize easily you can actually see these

Figure 6

figures. If you don't, you can simply sense them, or tell yourself that they are there. Let the mind dwell on each form: the square, the triangle, and the circle. Imagine the square as Order, the triangle as Balance and the circle as Harmony. Repeat the words, Order, Balance, and Harmony to yourself. After spending a few moments with these images, allow them to dissolve away into golden light. They become fluid golden light that flows around you and into you, surrounds you and permeates you. Repeat to yourself the word Flow. This is the light and warmth of life, the vital life force. It is the light of the sun. It supports, strengthens and nourishes you. Perhaps the geometric configurations become a wave, or a spiral. Allow that wave to flow over you and into you. Breathe it in, feel the energy of it. The Order of the universe, of health, is not some fixed and static state. It is a flow coalescing into form, moving through and in form (Figure 6).

•

SourcePoint teaches you to work with the mandala of the body. Explore this precious, unique mandala. Healing is an art, and you are the artist.

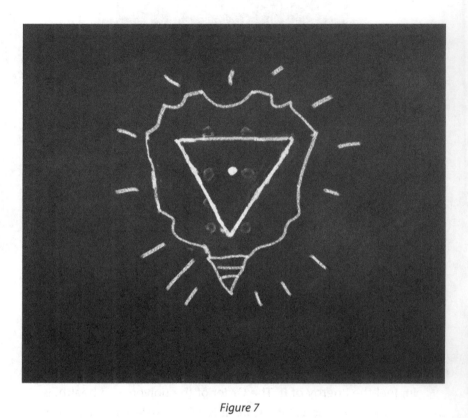

Figure 7

CHAPTER FOUR

Sacred Bone: The Sacrum

You have the sun within you
but you keep it knotted up
at the base of your spine.

—Rumi

THE INNER TEMPLE has its gateways and guardians. We enter this sacred ground with care. We approach it with respect, honoring the light within. The sacrum is the main entrance to the Inner Temple on the physical plane.

In ancient times the sacrum was called the sacred bone. The word sacrum comes directly from the Latin *Os sacrum*, which in turn was derived from the Greek *Hieron Osteon,* with still deeper roots in the Egyptian mystery schools where the sacrum was associated with Osiris, the god of resurrection. The Greek word *Heiron* meant not only sacred but also temple. Because of its size the sacrum is said to be often the last bone to rot when the body is buried. In ancient Egypt, it was considered the focal point around which the body would be re-assembled in the afterlife.

In Mesoamerican traditions as well as Old World cultures, the sacrum was related ritually and in iconography to reproduction, fertility and reincarnation. It was a portal permitting the movement of shamans and spirits between the worlds. [27]

The sacrum is a downward pointing triangular bone at the base of the spine made up of five vertebrae, which fuse between the ages of eighteen and thirty. The sacrum functions as a keystone in the arch formed by the legs and the pelvis. The Oxford English Dictionary defines the sacrum as:

"A composite, symmetrical, triangular bone which articulates laterally with the illia, forming the dorsal (back) wall of the pelvis and resulting from the ankylosis (fusion) of two or more vertebrae between the lumbar and coccygeal regions of the spine." [28]

In early Goddess figures there is often a downward-facing triangle traced on the front and back of the figures, symbolizing generative power, delineating both the womb and the sacrum as the seat of that power. In the Taoist tradition the sacrum is referred to as the Immortal Bone, the seat of Yuan Qi, the energy of incarnation. It is the junction point of heaven and earth energies, just as it joins the two sides of the pelvis and the upper and lower body. It is also considered to be a direct link to the original essence.

The sacrum is a gateway between the energetic domain and the physical structure of the human body. When we work with the sacrum, we are evoking the primal life force energy of the body as well as the information of the Blueprint. We support and nourish the physical body with the sacred fire of that vital energy.

In our experience, work with the sacrum re-awakens the elemental memory of the body's evolution and connection to all life that has come before. When we work with the sacrum, we are working with that which is deep and primal, the force of physical incarnation. The roots of the word *incarnation* mean literally "in flesh." From the SourcePoint perspective we are all spirit incarnate. The diffuse energy of Source, guided by the information of the Blueprint, contracts, coalesces into a certain energetic pattern and structure, and emerges into form. Incarnation is that process of contraction and manifestation.

Our bodies carry the memory of incarnation. The energy centers of the body known by the Sanskrit word *chakras* are energetic structures that constitute the midline around which the energy of the body organizes. Traditionally the root, or first chakra, holds that core contraction of incarnation: survival issues and primal fear relating to the material world and survival in it. The second chakra, which encompasses the pelvic and sacral area, is said traditionally to relate to issues of self-expression, individuation, sexuality, and repressed emotion. Therefore, when we work with the sacrum, we work with deep forces of survival and fear, life in the material world, personality and emotion.

From the SourcePoint perspective the sacrum is the focal point around which the body in its present incarnation is organized. In the drawing of the Vitruvian man surrounded by the Diamond Points (Figure 5) the Navel Point is the energetic center of the body, and the sacrum is the geometric center. We work at an energetic level with the sacrum directly to open the gateway for the information of the Blueprint to move more freely on the physical plane. The energetic structure of the sacrum is delineated by a set of points we call the Sacral Diamond, the center of which is the Sacral Point first mentioned in Chapter Two. Working with these points can help to strengthen the energetic armature of the vulnerable sacral area. In SourcePoint there are also specific Sacral Holds that nourish this area and support its vitality.

In many spiritual and healing traditions the sacrum is considered to be the seat of the sacred force of Kundalini, the yogic life force energy. According to the teachings of these traditions, as this force is released the individual consciousness is freed from its bondage to the perception of individual being and moves towards a larger perception, an experience of itself as Divine. However, from the SourcePoint perspective we work with the sacrum to support you, body, soul, essence and spirit, on your journey in time and space, in this material world, in this incarnation, to realize your full potential here on this earth.

Indeed, this sacred bone deserves our attention, recognition and respect! Take a moment now to sit with the basic meditation with the breath you learned in Chapter One, allowing the breath to relax into the sacral/pelvic area, what is called in Oriental Medicine the Hara, the soft belly, extending from the sternum into the lower abdomen. Relax that area. Breathe gently, feeling the breath fill the space, experiencing the inhalation and exhalation. Be aware of the sacrum. Don't force anything, just breathe and allow energy to move. Honor this seat of the soul, the gateway to the inner temple, this lovely triangle of a bone that supports you daily in moving through your life (Figure 7).

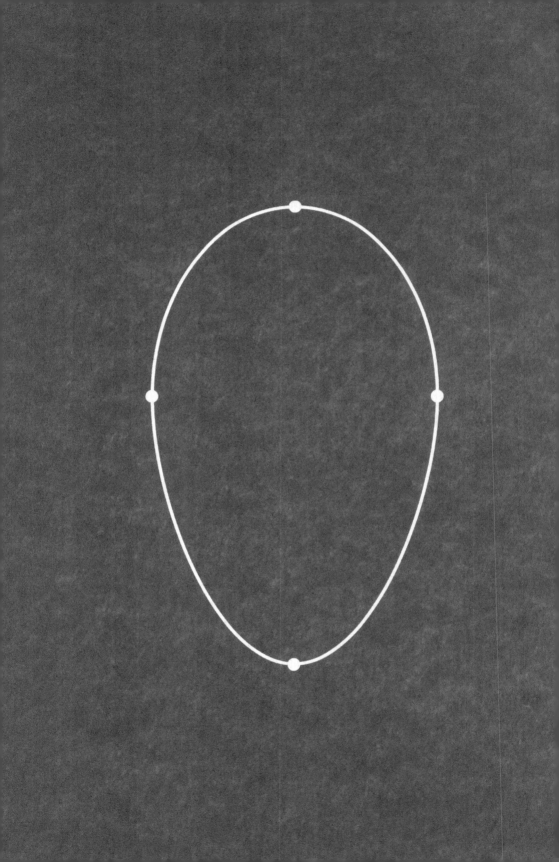

CHAPTER FIVE

The Guardians of the Body

Protecting oneself, one protects others. Protecting others, one protects oneself.

—The Buddha

HAVE YOU EVER felt a sudden drop in your energy level right after walking into a roomful of people? Can you remember walking into a place and immediately feeling exhausted? Have you ever been crammed into a crowded airplane with the person next to you coughing and sneezing for the entire ten-hour flight? Do you wake up at night and have trouble returning to sleep? Do you need confidence for a job interview or to make a special presentation at an important meeting? Do you feel your energy drained by the people you work with—or live with? Are you burnt-out and stressed? As a practitioner of the healing arts, do you over-identify with your clients and feel you sometimes take on their energies?

When faced with challenging situations such as these, know that you can activate the Guardians of the Body to protect yourself and to restore your energy.

Who or what are these protectors and how do we access them?

The archetype of the Guardian is found throughout human history. He or she appears in dreams, at the entrances to temples and cathedrals, in shamanic ritual and healing practices. Indigenous healers have their allies in the spirit world. For centuries, people have called upon deities, saints, spirits and angels for healing and protection. Guardianship is an ancient principle of spirituality and healing.

From the SourcePoint perspective, the ultimate Guardian of the Body is the Blueprint of health, and connecting to the Blueprint can be an important step in protecting yourself. However, let's examine this principle of Guardianship more closely and explore the many ways of working with it directly on a daily basis to sustain our health and well-being. There are three levels of Guardianship: spiritual, mental and physical. All have their place. See what resonates for you.

THE SPIRITUAL LEVEL OF GUARDIANSHIP

The Guardian may appear to people as an angel, a spirit animal, a spirit guide, or a deity. I keep a candle in the small, arched window by my front door. On its glass container a guardian angel is depicted. You may have seen this very popular image: an angel hovers over two small children who are crossing a rickety bridge that hangs precariously above a rocky gorge and a rushing river. Our lives are full of precipices, dangerous moments, turning points and choices. Most of the time we cross through these as the children on the bridge do—happily unaware of the dangers, not realizing the unseen protection we have. As we become more aware of our connection to Source, we also become more aware of the guardian energies within it.

It's not necessary to relate to guardian angels specifically in order to connect with the guardian energies at this spiritual level. There are many other ways to experience that great universal healing energy that guides and protects us. However, I have seen and felt great beings of light hovering near, radiating love and light. So have many others. For example, Bob's mother was ill with toxemia during her last few days of her pregnancy and after he was born she was very close to death. Her body was shutting down and her kidneys weren't functioning. Penicillin was just coming into widespread use and the attending physician gave her a dose. After doing so, the doctor turned to Bob's grandmother and said, "It's not up to me any more; it's up to God." Bob's mother heard this and drifted off into sleep. She awoke in the night to see a Guardian Angel hovering above her bed, beautiful and reassuring. She began to recover. The next morning her kidneys and all her other systems were functioning; the doctor was amazed at her unprecedented sudden recovery. She has always remembered her Guardian Angel and loves to tell the story.

Just before the actual moment of my own mother's death, I saw the light leave her body and join a greater light that filled the room. The hospice nurse later told me that many people had shared such stories with her. This great guardian light comes to people with different faces and forms; it is given many names and people tell their own unique stories about it. We find a common theme in all the stories. There is a light, a healing power in this universe that guides you. It helps you. You can call on it. Evidently it isn't all-powerful. People are injured; they die. And yet—as it would seem from the stories people have told for millennia—the light is there, in its myriad forms, to protect people, to give the gift of healing, to bring peace to people in their injury or illness, and to guide them in their dying. In times of extremity, you can call upon this light for help. As you receive this light, it is naturally accompanied by love—for yourself, for others and for the world you live in. You feel loved and cared for. You naturally want to take care of yourself. You want to be of service to others. This is the spiritual level of Guardianship.

THE MENTAL LEVEL OF GUARDIANSHIP

At this level, the mind can be a powerful ally—or an equally powerful enemy. As we all know, the mind can go around in wheels of obsessive worry and fear, self-judgment and blame, despair and doubt. Or it can rest in stillness and centeredness, acceptance and awareness, clarity and compassion. Why not put it to work for you? The previously dismissed placebo effect has recently been the subject of scientific study. Lo and behold, it turns out the mind does affect healing! The book *Timeless Healing: The Power and Biology of Belief,* by Herbert Benson, MD, is a classic on this subject. He uses the term *Remembered Wellness* rather than placebo effect to describe the positive effects of thoughts and beliefs on healing.[29] This term gives you power. The term placebo effect implies that there was nothing really wrong physically to begin with. *Remembered Wellness* acknowledges there is a real problem, but implies that you have the choice to focus your attention on your innate wellness, on the funda-mental health of your body, or that of your client, even as you attend to illness. You can use your mind to help heal the body. You are not powerless.

It doesn't mean it's all up to you, that if you do enough mental exercise you can totally cure yourself of everything. It means exactly what I have said: *your mind can be your ally. Your mind can be a Guardian of the Body.*

One of the functions of a guardian is to, at times, restrict your activities. Wise parents put loving limits on their children in many ways, even while encouraging them to explore. Your conscious mind, your awareness, often acts in this same way. The more you listen to yourself, the more protected you are. Your body often demands that you limit yourself in order to heal: you need to choose carefully your activities, what you eat, how you spend your time. You need to listen to the inner voice that tells you to get some rest, to take some time off, to start exercising. That's a Guardian of the Body speaking to you.

Your intuition, an aspect of your awareness, is also a valuable ally. It's related to that wise voice that limits you. Your intuition tells you a certain person, place, or thing isn't really good for you. You ignore that intuitive voice, and regret it moments, months, or years later. It's a long process to come to a place where you can trust intuition. You first have to learn to clear yourself of hope and fear, and be in a still, neutral place when you listen. Then that intuition lets you know with considerable accuracy what to avoid and what to embrace from day to day, and you recognize it as your inner Guardian. This is awareness, the mental level of guardianship.

THE PHYSICAL LEVEL OF GUARDIANSHIP

The body has its own intelligence, which acts as its Guardian. Scientists are beginning to perceive the body as a network of energy and information relating to a larger network. It is no longer viewed as fixed entity acted on by outside forces. To quote Candace Pert: "This view of the organism as an information network departs radically from the old Newtonian mechanistic view... With information added to the process, we see that there is an intelligence running things. It is not a matter of energy acting on matter to create behavior but of intelligence in the form of information running all the systems and creating behavior." [30]

At the physical level, the body's precious, wise Guardian is the immune system. Most of us are familiar with the military model of the immune system, where inner forces battle outside invasion. Today, there is beginning to be a shift away from that view. As Fritjof Capra says, "The entire system looks much more like a network, more like people talking to each other, than soldiers out looking for enemy." [31]

So, researchers are discovering that the Guardian systems of the body are talking to and communicating with invading energies rather than battling them! This is a very different story from the one scientists were telling a few years ago. Hearing this new story, we begin to really understand what we need to do to protect our health. The Guardian *activities* of the body are *communication, movement, flow, connection, and expression.* These are the essential actions or behaviors of a healthy organism. Studies show that the immune system is suppressed by depression, isolation, and stress. It is brought into healthy balance by experiences of happiness, community, social activity, and positive states of mind. Exercise strengthens your immune system, and so does meditation. (Again, if you want to know more about this, even a little Internet research on this topic will yield much valuable information.) By engaging in activities that support a balanced, strong immune system, you can experience greater energy and health. This is the physical level of guardianship.

Returning to the perspective of SourcePoint Therapy, we consider the Blueprint to be the ultimate Guardian of the Body. In addition to the Diamond Points, which directly connect to the Blueprint, there are special Guardian Points that further activate the Guardian energies of the body. The Guardian Points operate to stimulate communication and flow within the body, further integrating the information of the Blueprint. Working with these points helps to repair the broken links of the body's energetic information network and opens the channels of communication between this network and the Blueprint. People find the Guardian Points to be powerful tools for self-help; they organize and strengthen the individual energy field in response to disruption or invasion of any kind, whether physical, mental, emotional or psychic.

The Guardian Points not only restore your energy, they also defend, but not in the manner of a soldier doing battle. When activated, they can work at the energetic level to filter out and transmute disruptive and unwanted energy in a person's energy field before it has a chance to manifest as ill health at the physical level.

When you invoke the guardians of the body, you are focusing your attention on strengthening and stabilizing your energy, with the intention of supporting your health. You are involved in your own health and wellbeing in a proactive, positive way.

You don't work with the guardians of the body instead of taking whatever steps needed at the physical level. People need to pay attention to their immune system and protecting themselves at the physical level according to their chosen medical guidance and their own research and understanding. Again, these SourcePoint practices provide a ground, a container and a support for what you do at the everyday physical level.

The Guardian Points can be used very effectively for self-help but it is necessary to be precise and clear about the location of the points. We teach them in Module Two of SourcePoint Therapy. Practitioners who have learned to work with these points can also teach them to their clients. Remember, however, that you can invoke the Guardians of the Body by working with the Diamond Points, as you have already learned, and also by practicing the variation with the Golden Egg described below. Just becoming aware of the different levels of guardianship that we have discussed in this chapter can support you in recovering and maintaining connection to the Guardians of the Body. Remember another fundamental principle of SourcePoint: *There are Guardians of the Body that protect, nourish and strengthen us, bringing greater Order, Balance, Harmony and Flow into our lives. We can access these Guardians for the benefit of our health and that of others.*

Here is a message from the Guardians for you: You are not alone. When you are ill or in pain, you are not alone. Invoke the Guardians of the Body. Ask them for support. When you seek help and guidance for yourself, it comes. When you work with another's illness and pain, the Guardians are there. A great network of healing energy nourishes and supports life on this earth. Everywhere you go, in everything you experience, support is always there. And remember, the Blueprint of health is a great resource, a strong Guardian.

THE GOLDEN EGG: A MEDITATION

•

Imagine those Guardians however you like. Maybe you tune into the myriad biochemical mechanisms that protect you daily. Maybe you visualize guardian angels, or feel yourself surrounded by rainbow light or white light. How do you experience the Guardians of the Body? Contemplating this question is the first phase of this meditative practice.

Then, lie back, close your eyes, tune into the Order, Balance, Harmony and Flow of your breath, and imagine the Diamond Points around you. Imagine a golden line connecting the points, outlining an oval, and feel yourself completely surrounded by an egg of golden light. Place your hands cupped over the navel area, with the palm of one hand over the navel and the other on top. Invoke the Guardians of the Body. Say out loud "I call upon the Guardians of the Body to protect and strengthen this body." Then visualize, feel, or in some other way connect with your imagery for the Guardians. Rest and breathe in that Golden Egg.

•

CHAPTER SIX

Scanning

*Transfixed by our technologies, we short-circuit the sensorial reci-
procity between our breathing bodies and the bodily terrain. Human
awareness folds in upon itself, and the senses—once the crucial site
of our engagement with the wild and animate earth— become mere
adjuncts of an isolate and abstract mind bent on overcoming an
organic reality that now seems disturbingly aloof and arbitrary.*

—David Abrams, *The Spell of the Sensuous*

WHEN BOB AND I moved to the edge of the northern New Mexico wilder-
ness in 1997, people warned me to never let my beloved cat, Midnight, go
outside. If I did, she would be lost to a coyote, owl, or other predator. I've
never believed in keeping a cat indoors, but I made a real effort to keep
her housebound for the first few weeks we were there. She meowed and
paced and howled continuously. Finally, much earlier than I had intended,
I made the decision to trust her. One morning I explained to her she could
be outside as long as it was light—but she had to come home at dark. This
was a new world full of coyotes and owls, I told her, and opened the front
door. She paused on the threshold, quivering, looking in every direction
and sniffing the air. She stepped over and paused again. Her whole body
was one unified sensing device. I could see her shiny black fur literally
trembling with energy. Another step, another pause, head lifted. She was
scanning this new territory. Her body radar was taking in every frequency.
Then she ran for the garden wall and was up on the roof in a moment. She
lived to be twenty years old in our valley, with a few close calls. She never
once left the house without scanning.

I know you've seen animals do this. We have the same innate ability to sense energy. Scanning is an intuitive ability and evolutionary survival skill we all possess; we've just forgotten how to use it. Bruce Lipton, author of *The Biology of Belief,* says, "...all organisms, including humans, communicate and read their environment by evaluating energy fields. Because humans are so dependent on spoken and written language, we have neglected our energy sensing communication system. As with any biological function, a lack of use leads to atrophy." [32]

Scanning gives us information that is difficult to obtain in any other way. Aboriginal people in Australia are said to be able to sense the presence of water deep in the earth without any sort of instrument. Their sensory ability hasn't atrophied. In SourcePoint work we use scanning to re-activate that natural intuitive act of sensing energy. Just as the Aborigine can perceive water underground, we can locate energetic blockages in the body that are impeding the flow of information from the Blueprint. Our hands are highly responsive sensing devices. As we pass them over the body we experience sensations that give us answers to the questions we pose. These days we are often told to listen to the body. Scanning gives us a way to do precisely that.

Setting aside your preconceived notions is a prerequisite for practicing the SourcePoint scans effectively. Bob says: *In scanning, the specificity of the question is of utmost importance, so compose your question carefully. Be aware, also, that one's unconscious questions, preferences and attitudes can have as much to do with the results as the conscious questions one holds. I was at a workshop a number of years ago with an acupuncture teacher who demonstrated that when using muscle testing to determine which herbs and supplements were best for a patient he could easily influence the results by changing his inner orientation. It is the same with scanning. Your inner orientation and state of being have a profound influence on the outcome of your inquiries and the result of your treatments.*

Therefore, to do the SourcePoint scans you let go of your personal ideas and opinions. Instead, you hold a very specific question and shift your orientation entirely to the Blueprint, regardless of your particular discipline. This makes it possible to really listen to the body and accurately sense the frequencies of the energy field.

In SourcePoint Therapy there are two main scans we work with: the Entry Point Scan and the Primary Blockage Scan.

THE ENTRY POINT

One of the most important things a practitioner can do is establish trust and rapport with the client. The Entry Point Scan can be a significant aid in that trust-building process. In SourcePoint we begin a session by silently asking the question: "Where is the most appropriate entry point for this system at this time?" And then we scan the body by passing the hand, held in a specific position, lightly above the body until that spot is located. There is a specific sensation associated with discovering the entry point. Contact is then made at that point. Clients generally find that contact comforting and relaxing, and the scan itself is often experienced as soothing. Bob says of the scan: *The clients' bodies know deeply that your intention in touching them is good, and that you are taking the time to listen closely to their whole system. This alone is a significant therapeutic intervention, and an important point of your session regardless of what else you may do.*

The practice of the entry point can be applied in many situations. If you are a healthcare practitioner who hasn't yet studied and learned these SourcePoint methods, you can still think about the entry point when you meet your client. You are probably already aware that the beginning of each session is important. Your attitude, intention and how you approach the person sets the tone for the rest of the work you do, either supporting it or detracting from it. To approach a person with care and respect, focused on their needs and concerns, rather than carrying a preconceived opinion of how to proceed with them, sets a positive context for your work together.

The idea of the entry point can be useful also in everyday life. Situations and relationships all have natural entry points. It's a good approach to bring to any difficult or conflicted situation. Instead of just reacting, or plunging in with your ideas, opinions and emotions, step back. Take a look at the situation from the SourcePoint perspective. Ask yourself: *What's the best entry point into this situation? How do I connect with this person in the way they would most like to be connected with?* See what information comes to you and let it guide you. In this way the entry point naturally becomes a part of the way you view and interact with the world, even if you haven't yet learned the scanning technique.

THE PRIMARY BLOCKAGE SCAN

In a basic SourcePoint session, once we have located the entry point and made contact there, the next step is to scan for blockages. With this scan, we are looking for only one thing, asking only one question: *Where is the primary blockage that is obstructing the flow of information from the Blueprint?* We are not attempting to diagnose or treat any particular disorder in the physical body. Instead, our intention is focused on discovering energetic blockages.

In performing this scan, we relate to the physical body as an energy structure, a body of light. In SourcePoint we don't make a distinction between the physical body and the energy body. It's all one. So you are scanning the energy field and the physical body because the physical body *is also energy.* To work with the physical body is to work with energy; to work with the energy field is to work with the physical body. In addressing the blockages that are found, SourcePoint draws on all levels of touch, from off-the-body work to light touch to deep work within the body, depending on what the situation calls for and the prior training of the practitioner.

When doing the scan for blockages, along with framing the specific question about the location of the primary blockage, you also hold the intention of bringing a greater level of order into the body. While scanning, you don't think in terms of organs, nerves, tissues, meridians, chakras, or systems of the body. You hold the question of the primary blockage while passing the hand lightly above the body, in a different position than was used for the Entry Point. That is all you need to do, though to maintain that simplicity is not so easy.

People find that scanning takes practice. Bob has this to say about learning and practicing the Primary Blockage Scan: *I simply made a choice at some point to scan everyone that came into my practice. I did this for two years before I felt comfortable with it and that I was perceiving accurately. So remember, you are learning a skill that takes time, just like learning to play the piano or a new language takes time. There is the "10,000 hypothesis" which says it simply takes 10,000 hours of practice to learn anything well, be it running, tennis, an instrument or a language. Healing work in general, or your particular chosen discipline, is no different. Time and dedication and discipline are necessary. The great jazz pianist Keith Jarrett still practices every day, basic simple scales and basic structured practice. Personally I have been engaged in some form of dowsing for 40 years. I feel that it has taken at least thirty of those years to get to a place where I feel that I am relatively accurate eighty-five percent of the time. Sit quietly for a couple of minutes with your client before doing anything. Develop a way that you can check with yourself as to whether or not you are clear enough to scan accurately; you will get an inner sense of what that feels like. Withdraw projections, and have a very clear and accurate inquiry in mind.*

Once the blockage has been found, you proceed to address it by bringing the information of the Blueprint to the blockage. Learning to do this is a primary focus in all our workshops, at all levels.

Even if you have learned a scanning technique in a different healing modality, we ask that you do not try these specific scans before receiving training in them. The effectiveness of the SourcePoint scans comes from their precision and specificity. There are different hand positions for each of the scans, and different sensations we are looking for. The SourcePoint scans require training and practice, but you can apply the SourcePoint principles of clear and accurate inquiry, and withdrawal of projections, to any type of scan you do.

THE INNER SCAN: A MEDITATION

There is an inner scanning technique you can work with to enhance your ability to sense energy. This is a simple exercise, based on a traditional *Vipassana* (Insight) meditation. It teaches you how to go through the body in a certain way, noticing what is there without getting involved in it. Often in doing a scan people will sense what they think might be the blockage and then have the immediate reaction of wanting to do something about it. Instead you note it, pass it by, and make sure there isn't another even stronger one elsewhere. Only then do you do what needs to be done to release the primary blockage.

This Inner Scan meditation teaches you to notice and move on, without reactive intervention. It's great training for learning and practicing the SourcePoint scans; it develops the capacity to observe without interference. When you can do this within yourself, it will be much easier with another person. It's also relaxing and calming. In today's busy world it helps you to stay in touch with yourself and listen to your body.

•

To practice the Inner Scan, sit or lie down quietly, attune to your breath and breathe in and out for a few minutes, noting the arising of thoughts and returning your attention to your breath. Then, beginning at the top of the head, bring your attention to different parts of your body, working downward in whatever way feels right to you. Notice as you go where there is tension, blockage, discomfort and so on. Simply note it and move on, returning to the focus on the breath for a few seconds if you find yourself distracted or involved in thoughts about what you are experiencing.

As you move through the body, you may experience some natural release. You may notice some areas of tension or blockage, but do not try to adjust or change anything. Just open yourself to whatever occurs naturally. If you like, when you are done with the entire scan, you can return to the areas where you noticed tension, and breathe into them, or just sit quietly with them, holding them with your loving attention. Be aware again of the release that may naturally occur.

•

The practice of scanning brings us over and over to the question: "What do I need to do, what changes do I need to make in my life, in order to be a clearer observer?"

Right now, that simple question can begin to transform you, guiding you into a deeper awareness and clarity in your life. From Bob once again: *Through scanning you will eventually be able to find that which is at first elusive. It will yield riches that otherwise would have remained hidden.*

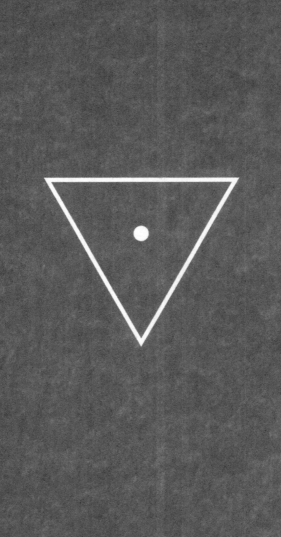

CHAPTER SEVEN

Getting Out of the Way

Agnes's and my art share a love of the anonymous, of doing the work. The work itself is what's important. We don't want our personality in the art. We all had to get over Picasso, because his was great 'personality art.' For abstract expressionists, gesture was very important—we were trying to get away from the 'I,' as in 'look how well I do it.' Then, there is a stillness we appreciate in each other's work, as in a common destiny.

—Ellsworth Kelly, *3X Abstraction, A New Method of Drawing*

AS WE CONNECT with the Blueprint for health, as we hold the points, as we practice SourcePoint Therapy—it's not about us. The statement above by Ellsworth Kelly, speaking of his and Agnes Martin's work, beautifully expresses the SourcePoint principle of *getting out of the way*. It's not about "personality healing." It's about the work. It's about the love of the anonymous and the willingness to be invisible. Malidoma Somé, in his book *Of Water and the Spirit*, tells us that true power remains hidden. [33] It doesn't display itself. It doesn't need to, and indeed is all the more powerful for being hidden. Anonymity, invisibility, and emphasis on the work rather than personality; all of this goes against the prevailing cultural norms. Our culture values personality and celebrity. And yet, to work deeply with energy, these can't be your primary concerns.

From the SourcePoint perspective, this chapter is crucial for those who wish to deepen their understanding and practice of energy work in any modality. SourcePoint methods offer excellent opportunities for learning to get out of the way and let the greater Order work. In this chapter we will focus on this theme specifically for people who practice, or wish to practice, energy work. However, the principles and practices are applicable in every area of our lives.

To devote oneself to working with energy, consciousness and healing is in fact a challenging spiritual path. All spiritual paths require you to let go of the ego, of the attachment to a personal point of view, of the sense of self that theoretically knows what is best for everyone. Working with energy demands all this of any practitioner, whether you are doing it for yourself or another. So often in life we get in our own way. We put up roadblocks, erect barriers, and make the possible impossible. Serving the universal healing energy, being its instrument, requires stepping aside. This doesn't mean you go unconscious and disappear. On the contrary, you allow your knowledge, your experience, your vocabulary and your whole body-mind to be utilized to support health and well-being in yourself or in another.

SourcePoint is not about becoming a miracle worker. It's about holding in your heart the intention to align with the essential Order, Balance, Harmony and Flow at every moment. This is not some abstract ideal. It can happen! However, no one is expecting you to become a saint. As you seek greater alignment with your true nature, you will go in and out of alignment and connection. Sometimes you will feel supported and part of a loving whole, while in other moments you may feel alone, disconnected and separate. The awareness within you lets you know when you are off and guides you back. Over and over it's the return that counts, not whether you got lost momentarily.

Getting out of the way does not imply sacrificing your own individual uniqueness. It is not about completely eradicating your personal likes and dislikes, your ideas and opinions. In fact, doing this work will help you to see clearly the belief systems, preferences and judgments you hold and accept them as simply that. You do not have to be controlled by them. *You do not give up your awareness.* In the practice of energy work, as in life, that awareness tracks and evaluates what happens, guides you, helps you determine if you are moving in the right direction. That's good. The challenge is to let the appropriate response occur, rather than jumping to what you think is the conclusion. Energy work requires great patience. To be able to sit with what is: this is one of the great skills of a compassionate person. Getting out of the way does not mean being absent. On the contrary, it allows you to be fully present. And that Presence in itself can be healing.

How then do you get out of the way of yourself? How do you become a mirror, reflecting your truest, deepest self to yourself, reflecting the person you encounter who needs help? And how do you do this without drama, without feeling special about it—which then just gets in the way? The practices of SourcePoint Therapy will help you with this. When you learn to hold the points for another person with the intention of bringing in the information of the Blueprint, you personally are not doing anything except holding the points. The more you focus on this one simple task, the easier it becomes to get out of the way. You are not channeling, you are not sending energy, you are not contacting anything; you are not healing anyone. You are simply holding the points. The points make the connection: information and energy flow to the body through *them*, not you. The Blueprint does the work. You are facilitating the connection of the person to the Blueprint. That's it.

The same is true when you are meditating with the points. You don't have to think about them or try to figure out what is or isn't happening. You just give your full attention to the points, one by one.

As you practice getting out of the way, don't start judging yourself. Don't get into a battle with what is commonly called the ego. In Source-Point work, we aren't trying to eliminate our egos or encouraging others to do so. On the path of energy medicine, the self discovers its wondrous true nature: that it belongs to a great universal energy, that it is always nourished and sustained by that energy, that love and awareness arise naturally from that experience of Wholeness. The ego is transformed and finds new meaning in a different experience of self. As we explore the principles and practices of SourcePoint, we find we are engaged not in the elimination of ego, but in the creation of a conscious self.

Be aware that it is impossible to get completely out of the way. There is no such thing as being one hundred percent clear. Truth and humility demand this acknowledgement. At every moment you are bringing your own vocabulary, understanding and experience to every situation. If you think you are one hundred percent out of the way, you can be sure you are not. If you think there is no ego in your work or in your relationships with others, you can be sure there is. If a healer or teacher says they have completely transcended ego, be careful of that person.

THE TRIAD

Of the many SourcePoint exercises that facilitate getting out of the way, the most important is *The Triad* (Figure 8). It is the foundation for working with others from the SourcePoint perspective and is useful in relationships of all kinds. It can be especially useful when you feel pulled or overwhelmed by another's energy. *In SourcePoint, the therapeutic relationship is not a dyad but a triad consisting of the Blueprint, practitioner, and client.* This is another fundamental principle of SourcePoint Therapy.

Figure 8

•

To practice this principle of the Triad, try the following. First imagine the Gold Point in the heart center of the other person you are relating to, whether a client, loved one, friend, or someone with whom you have a conflicted relationship. Then imagine that Gold Point in your own heart. Each of those points is connected to the Eight-Pointed Star above you both, as in a triangle. Imagine a golden line of light connecting each point to the star (Figure 8).

The connection is not directly heart-to-heart; it is heart-to-heart through the Eight-Pointed Star, which radiates the clear energy, light and information of the Blueprint and is an ordering, balancing and harmonizing presence.

•

If you are a practitioner engaged in healing work, you can be aware of this Triad as a focus for your attention when you work. Personally, you can use this in meditation. You can utilize the Eight-Pointed Star as a representation of the Blueprint, or you can also just imagine a Gold Point of light in each location. Whatever symbol you choose, it is the placeholder for the information of the Blueprint. The important thing is that you are connecting to the other person through the Order, Balance, Harmony and Flow of the Blueprint, and your attention is focused primarily on the Blueprint.

Practitioners find this practice helps them to maintain their energy; they report feeling less drained at the end of a day's work. Whenever you give a SourcePoint session, you are receiving the benefit of the Blueprint also!

A balance of compassion and detachment makes for effective work with others and this exercise helps develop just that: balanced compassion. As we work with this practice, we open our hearts to the healing power of unconditional love and acceptance and connect to others through that. We humbly acknowledge that we are not the source of this unconditional Love. *The nature of the Blueprint is Love.* It exists to nurture and sustain the unique and precious life of each individual being—and that is what Love does.

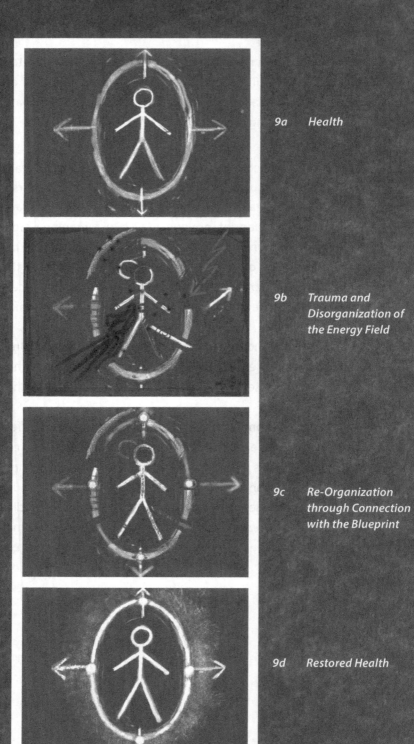

9a   *Health*

9b   *Trauma and Disorganization of the Energy Field*

9c   *Re-Organization through Connection with the Blueprint*

9d   *Restored Health*

Figure 9

CHAPTER EIGHT

Trauma

Trauma is a fact of life. It does not, however, have to be a life sentence. Not only can trauma be healed, but with the appropriate support and guidance, it can be transformative.

—Peter Levine, *Waking the Tiger*

AS WE SET about writing this book, we made an important discovery—that SourcePoint is essentially an oral tradition. We discovered we couldn't teach SourcePoint in a book. We tried. We began with the intention of including much more self-help and even thought we could show in the book how to do the basic points for others. It just didn't work. It is our belief that to go deep into the practice of energy work—to really experience and understand the nature of the forces we are working with—personal connection, training and guidance are required. Just as no two clients are the same, no two students are the same. And the principles and practices, while simple enough to learn in a few weeks of training, are profound enough to require a lifetime of continued exploration.

There are three modules in the SourcePoint Therapy training. In Modules One and Two, we learn to work with the points, the scans, the blockages, the energetic structures and the Guardians, all the principles and practices we have introduced you to so far.

In Module Three, our practice of SourcePoint progresses to the advanced level. In Module Three, and then more deeply in the Advanced Intensives, we learn to work with profound and complex energy-information patterns that may affect us at deep unconscious levels, such as trauma, karma and others. At this point in the book, we move into an introduction to these more advanced principles and practices. What we are able to share with you here is the general SourcePoint perspective on trauma and karma as factors that can affect our health and well-being. In this chapter we will explore the SourcePoint definition of trauma and the principles that can be applied in working with it at the energetic level.

We all carry our wounds, physical, emotional, and even spiritual. Some are recent, others are as ancient as time, passed down from generation to generation. Our individual energy fields bear the scars of our previous experience, as surely as our physical body does. Most of us have some awareness of these shadows of the past. They lie just below the edge of memory, or they may dominate our conscious mind. Often we relive these old memories over and over in painfully etched detail.

Whether we are conscious of them or not, the brain, body, spirit and heart hold memories, and these imprints of prior experience can inhibit the flow of the life force energy. How do we address memories that are affecting our health? Experience teaches that a single release isn't enough. Catharsis alone does not heal, and while telling the story is important, more is often needed.

From a SourcePoint perspective, trauma disorganizes and fragments the individual energy field. Facilitating the connection to the Blueprint and bringing greater order to that energy field is, in our view, a necessary foundation that will support any other therapeutic work with trauma. As always, in SourcePoint we are not trying to "heal trauma." We are working to restore the natural balance of the individual energy field.

The underlying principle here is that the Blueprint is also a memory and the body-mind-spirit holds this remembrance just as strongly as it holds the memories of trauma. Deep within, we remember the Order, Balance, Harmony and Flow from which we originally arose. As consciousness incarnates into material form, however, this memory dims. This is our original trauma: as we individuate and come into incarnation, there is a sense of separation. We lose our memory of Source.

As we experience this trauma, and all others that occur in our existence in the material world, the body forgets its inherent order because the individual energy field becomes disorganized. Our consciousness fragments and cannot find its center. We suffer. Everything that we call trauma—pain, injury, illness, accident, loss, grief, abuse, stress, violence, oppression, war, assault—can result in disconnection, disorganization, distress, and fragmentation in our energy fields. From the SourcePoint perspective, recovery from trauma involves reconnection to the Whole, to the deeper memory of health, to the information of Order, Balance, Harmony and Flow present in the Blueprint (Figure 9).

It is, of course, important to address any specific trauma with an equally specific physical or psychological modality and, thankfully, these days there are excellent rehabilitating treatments available. There are many therapies that work with the body-mind to release and heal the history of trauma. However, from the SourcePoint perspective, there is still sometimes a missing piece. It seems it may be more difficult to heal from trauma, to dispel its far-reaching shadow, *without a repaired and strengthened connection to the Blueprint.*

SourcePoint works with the principle of re-introducing, over and over, the information of Order, Balance, Harmony and Flow to the individual human energy field impacted by trauma. This is not new information, only forgotten, blocked by traumatic experience and memory. With the re-introduction of the Blueprint information, the body can begin to re-integrate the primordial experience of love, balance, health, harmony, and peace, and to organize itself around that core memory rather than the memories of trauma.

When we address trauma from the SourcePoint perspective, the information of the Blueprint interacts with the information of trauma to foster recovery. People often can repress the story of their trauma, but on the other hand, they can end up telling it over and over. To tell the story is necessary and important, but it can sometimes eventually slow their recovery. In SourcePoint, we help people to ground themselves in a different story, the story of natural and inherent Order, Balance, Harmony and Flow—in other words, health.

The more we are grounded in the story of health, the more we are prepared to withstand traumatic events in the future. Ongoing connection to the Blueprint helps to strengthen and balance the whole system. The body relearns its ability to instantly connect itself to the information of Order, Balance, Harmony and Flow. This can allow trauma to pass through us more readily, without getting stuck in the body's memory. As we see in Figure 9, the Diamond Points re-establish the energetic boundary and the connection to the Blueprint, and the energetic structure of the Stick Figure provides a center around which the energies of the body can re-organize themselves.

Despite the greater attention to trauma in the medical establishment and society in general, there are realities of life in the modern world that complicate recovery from traumatic experience. In the past, people could readily experience the essential Order, Balance, Harmony and Flow of existence in the world around them because nature was a perfect expression of it. The healing energies of earth and sky, tree and river, star and stone, were readily available to all. The natural cosmic order provided ongoing support for dealing with the trauma inherent in life. In today's world, most people don't have the gift of being able to walk out their door and into the Blueprint. People live in greater separation from the natural world than ever before in human history. And, the earth itself is struggling to maintain its balance.

As our connection to the Blueprint through the natural world has become tenuous, the points provide an alternative way to connect to the underlying Order, Balance, Harmony and Flow that is not subject to disruption and disturbance. We need that connection, and if we can't find it in the world around us, we have to look deeper, wider, and further. Historically, the rituals of traditional cultures functioned to maintain the connection between the Universal Order and the order of the material world. SourcePoint also serves that same purpose. We seek to maintain the link to the cosmic order for the benefit of all beings on this planet, and the planet itself.

Because SourcePoint does not treat specific conditions, we do not offer a specific meditative exercise for working with trauma. The Breath Meditation and the Diamond Points Meditation focus on accessing and maintaining the natural Order, Balance, Harmony and Flow of the Body. The Diamond Points assist in reorganizing and stabilizing the individual energy field. The Golden Egg supports and nourishes. As you explore and

experience the different dimensions of SourcePoint practices, you find
what works to support the health of your unique mind, body and spirit.

CHAPTER NINE

Karma

If you want to know your past life, look into your present conditions.
If you want to know your future life, look into your present actions.

—Padmasambhava

I WOULDN'T DREAM of trying to answer definitively the question: *What is karma?* However, if you are an energy worker, you will undoubtedly encounter the issue of karma. At the very least you may be asked whether or not you believe in reincarnation and whether past lives affect present health. For that reason, a basic understanding of the principles of karma can help you in your practice of energy work and, potentially, in understanding yourself. Remember, this is only the SourcePoint perspective, derived from our studies and personal experience; it is only one of many ways to view the universe and the complex questions of causation and incarnation.

The word *karma* in Sanskrit literally means *volitional action*; in other words, action that is intended and comes from choice. Many people have the idea that karma is fate or punishment, or very literal cause and effect: because you do something bad in one lifetime you are fated in a subsequent lifetime to experience suffering. However, karma is not only about limitation and obstruction. The literal meaning of the word implies choice and choice implies the possibility of transformation.

The principle of karma is often used these days to explain almost everything, but this is an over-simplification. An early Buddhist view suggests that we live in a vast web of interacting causes and effects, forces, energies, actions and information. According to these Buddhist teachings, there is a fundamental cosmic order reflected in five different causal mechanisms.

Karma is only one of the *niyamas,* or causal mechanisms, at work in the universe. Natural disasters, for example, would be due to *uti niyama*, the laws governing the physical order of the universe, rather than to karma. *Bija Niyama* includes the laws of living matter, such as genes, cells, viruses, germs, and much more. *Dhamma niyama* is the spiritual or transcendent order, the spiritual laws governing ultimate reality. *Citta niyama* is mind, which the Buddha recognized as an essential force in causation. And *khamma nimaya* is karma: "the activity of transforming energy through intention, speech and action." [34]

Karma, then, is one of these causative factors at work in this world but not the only one. We can't fully control whether bad things happen by our virtuous or non-virtuous actions. *What we can do is attend to our own actions and our responses to events*. No matter how overpowering an external situation may be, we always have a choice as to how we respond. As we take responsibility for actions, as we purify our mind, speech and actions, our lives change. That change may or may not be immediately reflected in outer circumstances, but we can come to greater peace in our inner world.

While some people dismiss karma as a factor in illness, many spiritual healers take the opposite approach and focus intensively on "clearing karma." In SourcePoint we have a different perspective. It's not about clearing; it's about transforming. Karma can be described as a storehouse of our past experience, the accumulated information of all we have experienced in incarnation. In this we find resources as well as blockages. We find the possibility of transforming deep old patterns through the choices we make in our thoughts, speech and action on a daily basis.

In my work, spanning several decades, I have explored karmic issues with many individuals and looked at literally thousands of stories with them. I know from my experience that each person carries stories in their cells, bones, skin, blood and deep unconscious memory. There are echoes of the past in the present lifetime, often amazingly precise. In a certain sense, we're made of stories. We may transform our stories, but there is always a story.

In SourcePoint our primary focus is not on the personal story. We do not ignore it but we focus our primary attention on the story of health for the human being, which is held within the Blueprint, as is the story of our highest potential. As we connect with the Blueprint, this story of health interacts with the stories we carry from past experience to help bring about that transformation of old patterns.

Karma is awareness in action, choosing and creating. Therefore clearing karma depends on the choices we make in the present, and those choices depend on the degree of awareness we can bring to our lives. No healer can clear your karma. Only you can transform it. In SourcePoint we work always to strengthen the connection to the Blueprint, to bring the information of the Blueprint to energetic blockages, to restore natural Order, Balance, Harmony and Flow. That's what we are always doing with SourcePoint Therapy, no matter what cause, condition or pattern a person brings. From a greater foundation of Order, Balance, Harmony and Flow, it's possible for people to begin to make better choices. And that is the essence of the transformation of karma.

In any situation, we can ask: *What is my karma here?* That means: *What are my choices, what is the appropriate action?* As we begin to understand this we begin to transform the pattern of our experience. Karma is our blessed human birthright to choose, to weave a new pattern, to experience a different story. *It's about transformation.*

What about reincarnation? Let's explore this possibility, and again, use our imagination. SourcePoint works with pattern and information. From this perspective we could say that we each have a karmic blueprint. Just as the Blueprint of health for the human being is an energy pattern that transmits the information of Order, Balance, Harmony and Flow, so then our karmic blueprint would be the energy-information pattern that transmits the information of our prior experience. We can understand it as one factor that informs our unique physical/emotional/mental body at the moment of incarnation.

From here, we could hypothesize that as consciousness disperses at death, the imprints and patterns of one lifetime would be released into the great energy-information field we call Source. These patterns would then re-form and reincarnate, manifesting once again into physical form, in alignment with familiar genetic-biological patterns. Pattern is drawn to pattern, information to information.

This is another way to understand reincarnation and rebirth: as a process of energy and information constantly recreating itself into form. As new information comes in, in any given lifetime, the trajectory changes. Using the term Blueprint we can understand that form arises from interwoven layers of intersecting blueprints, templates, patterns and information. From this perspective, rebirth is not such a linear process as people often imagine. The dance of pattern, the melding and re-shaping of consciousness, is a constant process. Information doesn't go away; it changes according to causes and conditions. Information is constantly reborn into new forms. This seems to be the nature of the universe; why would human beings be any exception? At any given moment the state of the body-mind is arising from and connected to countless stories, intricate information.

When we hold or visualize the Diamond Points we strengthen the connection of our individual karmic/genetic blueprints to the universal Blueprint of health. We are reminding ourselves of our essential nature and highest potential. In connecting to the Blueprint we strengthen the presence of the universal Blueprint information in the body and shift the balance of power from the personal story to the larger story of Order, Balance, Harmony and Flow. Our focus shifts from our past history with its limitations and restrictions, to our future, with the possibility of realizing our full potential. That's the ground of transformation that supports us in making different choices.

Karma is an essential element of our human lives, one that we who practice SourcePoint work with carefully and consciously, honoring it as the path of our unique individual being, a path that opens before us as we grow in wisdom and compassion.

One simple, effective way to work with karma is to remember in any given situation: *I have choice.* Take time to see what your choices are. Very often your only choice may be in how to respond to the situation. Take advantage of that choice. Listen to the inner voice that says: *You don't have to go that way. You can go this way instead.* Remember that every action, every thought, every response, is a seed you sow, that blossoms and bears fruit in the future—or not. Again, we emphasize simplicity.

Take responsibility for your past life, your present life, and your future life. Don't use karma as an excuse. Accept it as a challenge: that which helps you grow, that which guides you. Karma is the power of awareness. To work with karma means to follow the ancient dictum: *Know Thyself.*

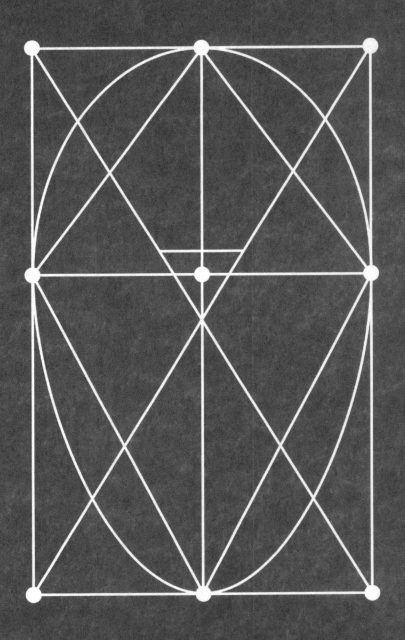

CHAPTER TEN

SourcePoint and Personal Transformation

I see how SourcePoint helps me love myself. When I experience myself, just as I am—as a beautiful mandala of light arising from the cosmic order—how can I not love such a self?

—Donna Thomson, *the Author*

SOURCEPOINT THERAPY PROVIDES you with specific energy work protocols, but SourcePoint is also a way of being in the world, a way of looking at the world. The principles and practices that we have explored so far can also guide you in your personal growth and transformation. It is possible to integrate them into your life at whatever level you choose.

SourcePoint as a way of being in the world involves a radical re-definition of self. As you become aware of the vast energy-information field in which you live, your perspective on yourself changes. You no longer experience yourself as isolated and separate, but rather as a unique manifestation of a cosmic Wholeness. That universal field in which you exist is not neutral. It is imbued with the energies of Order, Balance, Harmony and Flow and can be experienced as a steady, loving presence. As you strengthen your connection to that field, you become intimately aware of the support and guidance that is always available to you.

Inevitably, working with energy heightens your awareness and increases your sensitivity, bringing you into greater alignment with the fundamental Order, Balance, Harmony and Flow that is your original nature. Along this path of reunion, you may sometimes encounter experiences that feel like intensified imbalance, or conflict, or upheaval. In any process of inner transformation that goes deep, there's going to be a sense at times of disorientation, of not knowing exactly who you are. The old disappears and the new takes time to appear. There will be times of joy, conviction, even bliss. There will be times of doubt, confusion, and loss of identity. The constant throughout these shifting states is your awareness.

Focus on awareness and allow the landscape to shift, the old to release, and the new to appear. Recognize the underlying rhythm of these experiences: contraction, expansion, joy, sorrow, confidence, doubt, love, trust, expansion, contraction, and so on. Be patient and simply allow this rhythm to be. You will sometimes have the experience of union, followed by the intense experience of separation. This is the rhythm of the human experience in search of the greater Order, the Divine, meaning, peace, and spiritual growth. It is the rhythm of life itself.

When you are going through inner transformation your whole energy field is reorganizing itself. Meditation with the Diamond Points at such a time won't fully replace a more comprehensive spiritual practice but it can help to orient you, and help you stay connected to the Order, Balance, Harmony and Flow inherent in the Blueprint. The continued connection to the Blueprint as the Source of your unique being and the affirmation of it on a daily basis gives you a ground to stand on in the midst of change, a stable foundation in the midst of an unstable world.

In quantum physics we find the principle of the observer effect. Scientists have discovered that at the quantum level simply observing a phenomenon can bring about changes in it. Observation, which we can also call attention, is a powerful force in our universe, at every level. There is a story of a Zen master who was asked, "What is the Tao?" He replied "Attention! Attention! Attention!" This story is often told to impress upon eager students the importance of alert awareness in their meditation. However, it takes on new and different shades of meaning when we examine it more deeply, and when we practice attention in our everyday life. We come to understand that attention (observation, awareness, consciousness) has the power to transform our lives, and indeed is the very ground of our existence.

Most quantum physicists probably wouldn't be prepared to make this leap, but remembering the ancient dictum *as above, so below*, we might wonder if perhaps someday science will discover that what happens at that quantum level echoes throughout every dimension. I can easily make the leap to see that it is not only at the quantum level that the practice of observation is powerful and can produce change. I can see every day how what I pay attention to transforms the quality and direction of my life.

As soon as you focus your mind on the Source Point, you are observing the possibility of connecting to the Source of your being, connecting to the Blueprint of perfect health for the human body. If you work with the points on a regular basis, you will find that the Blueprint brings you information not only for the body, it brings the information your unique being needs for emotional and spiritual transformation as well. Order, Balance, Harmony and Flow begin to appear in your life.

When you bring your attention to the Grounding Point, you are observing yourself as a manifestation of the universal energy, grounded in your full potential. You honor your unique, unrepeatable being. At the same time, you are grounding yourself in the Blueprint, and therefore your fullest potential, rather than in all the stories you tell yourself about who you are. To hold the Grounding point for yourself, by focusing your mind on it, is a specific practice in loving yourself. People are often told to love themselves, but it's not so easy sometimes. Meditating with the Diamond Points, and this point in particular, is a practice in loving your unique self. Yes, you are living in the material world, and yet you do not forget the Source of your being. You are aware of your connection to it. You remember you are not separate from it.

When you observe the Activation Point with your awareness, you focus on action. In this material world, you act, you do, you communicate, you relate. When you observe this point in meditation you are working towards more harmonious action in the world, seeking to unify your action with the Source of your being, with the Order, Balance, Harmony and Flow of the universal energy. You come into alignment with that information more and more as you walk and talk and live in the world.

When you focus your attention on the Transformation Point, you are facilitating the creation of a conscious self; you are the midwife to the birth of that transformed self.

To focus on all these points is an act of choice, the choice to live consciously, in awareness, in alignment and connection with the Source of your being.

As you practice with the Diamond Points, as you meditate with them, as you enter into the energy of Order, Balance, Harmony and Flow, and *see those qualities as your fundamental nature,* this enhances your ability to make more choices that keep you in alignment, in balance. To live in alignment with this flow doesn't mean you always feel good; it doesn't mean you never have emotions that arise and cause disturbance. It doesn't mean everything always goes smoothly in your life. But it does mean that you are always supported, never alone; you are always grounded in your connection and you can always return to it. The information of the Blueprint begins to work in you more directly and continues to work in you.

As you work with these points you are aligning with the deep intention of the universal energy, of Source. Each one of the Diamond Points *is* an intention. The Diamond Points work to attune the vibration of the physical body to its Source. You may therefore find yourself changing your diet, changing your habits, changing your attitudes. You may find that your creativity is enhanced, that synchronicities appear more often in your life. Perhaps you experience a greater flow and a greater acceptance of what is. You may find yourself coming into contact with spiritual teachers or paths that resonate for you; you may change professions or relationships. Or, your outer life may continue to look exactly the same but you become aware of changes within. Healthcare practitioners who work with the Diamond Points for themselves as well as others tell us they are less tired at the end of the day. That connection to the Blueprint nourishes the practitioner also.

With SourcePoint, intention works from the depths to the surface. You can, of course, set goals and work towards them, but that's not what we're talking about here. Intention and goals are two different streams of energy. Goals are specific things you want to accomplish or manifest, whereas intention is the focused direction and flow of the universal energy expressing itself through you. As you remember the rhythm of Source, Grounding, Activation and Transformation, of Order, Balance, Harmony, Flow, you experience your deep intention as a force that carries you forward and takes you in those directions that you most need to go. It brings you the experiences you need. It assists you in setting goals that are attuned to your deepest self.

It is a natural process for you to realize your fullest human potential. It is the intention of the universal energy that gives rise to life that everything should manifest its fullest potential.

Sometimes people ask, how much difference does it make if I really believe all of this? Is belief important for transformation to take place? Belief from a SourcePoint perspective simply means being open to possibility. Belief in the fanatical sense can cause the mind and heart to close down and become narrow. This is not the kind of belief that brings greater health and wholeness. There is an alchemical process that happens in healing with the practice of connecting to the universal energy in one way or another. When you work with the points of SourcePoint Therapy and begin to consciously connect with the Source of your being, you express openness to the possibility of transformation. Stay open, and your physical-emotional-spiritual being can begin to transform.

You aren't transforming yourself; you are allowing yourself to be transformed. People like to feel they are in control of things, but in fact, spiritual growth and self-healing ask you to let go of the idea that you are in control. To feel that you have to believe certain things, or that you are blocking the process if you don't, implies that somehow you are still in charge. From a SourcePoint perspective, openness and receptivity are keys to transformation, and this is demonstrated by a dedicated persistence, an ongoing willingness to keep moving along your unique path. If despite all the doubts, questions, analysis, obstructions, setbacks you may experience, you regularly do a simple practice such as bringing your attention to Source, Grounding, Activation and Transformation, then that is faith—openness to possibility.

That said, we aren't putting forth SourcePoint as a way to enlightenment, a spiritual practice in and of itself, or a means of miraculous healing. Our intention is more modest. We see it is a *practical* practice of transformation, a way of working with energy that opens you to an inner transformation—which then helps you to follow your chosen spiritual path, to discover your tasks, to live from the Source of your being. It is not magic. It is one way among many of connecting to that greater information of Order, Balance, Harmony and Flow.

As you maintain your connection to the Blueprint you will become more aware of how to support your health at the physical level. In today's world, there are so many choices for treatments, from pills and surgery to pure energy work and spiritual healing. It can be confusing. Connection to the Blueprint can help to guide you to the physical modalities that you need. Do not ignore the physical world and its physical medicine. What works best in our times, from the SourcePoint perspective, is the integration of different modalities at different levels to address the different aspects of your being.

Using the Diamond Points throughout the day helps to recharge you, refresh you, and reconnect you. It can shift your energy and this can positively affect outer circumstances. Change begins with each one of us, always. We cannot force others to change. We can work with our own energy, intention, alignment and connection, and SourcePoint gives us one simple way to do that. The emphasis is on the word *simple*. Some of the theory may seem complex, but the points are simple. There isn't a lot to learn.

Health takes work. Health requires attention, and discipline, and awareness. The universal energies of Order, Balance, Harmony and Flow are always supporting us. We have to remember them, to focus on them, to work with them. Once we truly set our intention on health, that intention has an energy that carries us forward. Here is a reflection and meditation on the power of intention. Don't expect to remember every word, just read and absorb the spirit of the meditation, and then close your eyes and allow yourself to enter into a state of deep intention.

CONNECTING WITH YOUR DEEP INTENTION: A MEDITATION

Intention is not a matter of will. Deep intention is a flow of energy you align with, not something you decide to do. You are born with this deep intention imprinted in your cells. From the SourcePoint perspective you do not *set* intention; *you enter into it.* You connect with it. It is already there, waiting. You may not even know consciously what it is, but sitting quietly, you enter its flow, you begin to move with the wave, you experience being in the rhythm of that deep inherent intention. From the SourcePoint perspective there is no division between body and soul. The body is the expression of the soul and when aligned with its true nature, carries out the intention of the soul.

When you sit quietly, breathing, allowing the mind to settle and free itself from discursive thought, then there is space for that intention to work in you and through you. You link with your intention. The individual deep inherent intention that is your birthright is one with the deep inherent intention of the universal energy, the earth energy, the sky energy. You are never alone in your intention when you are aligned with yourself and therefore these greater energies. When you connect to the Blueprint through the Diamond Points, you are connecting with your deep intention.

•

So take a moment now, sit and bring your attention to your breath. Feel the breath rise and fall. Be aware of the inhalation and exhalation. Experience the rhythm of your own unique being. Imagine the Diamond Points around you.

- The Source Point to your right, at the level of the navel, about eighteen inches out from the body, a tiny golden seed of light

- The Grounding Point below your feet

- The Activation Point to your left side

- The Transformation Point above the head.

As you bring your attention to each point, you connect with your deep intention and it connects with you. Intention is a specific field of energy that you can align yourself with through inner silence and attention. Intention is a palpable presence; it is that which informs you. As you enter into it and dwell in it, goals, visions, desires, new directions may emerge.

Take a moment and feel this truth arising deep inside yourself: you know where you are going. Your whole being is imprinted with the knowledge of why you are here, where you are going and what you are doing. Allow yourself to settle into that knowing, silently, without words, simply by feeling your breath, being aware of your breath. You know. *You know.*

Allow yourself to let go of needing to know with your conscious mind. Instead, enter into the state of knowing beyond that mind. Rest in that wordless knowing that is your nature. The more you let go of the need to know in the usual sense, the more your inner knowing can manifest.

At this very moment, you are surrounded by intention, embraced by intention, filled with intention; you inhale intention and you exhale intention. This entire universe is an expression of intention: the intention to be, to manifest, to take form, give birth. You are a part of that. You are a manifestation of universal intention.

The deepest intention can never be put into words. It is simply there:

Be. Manifest. Arise. Live. Grow.

When you focus your mind you experience your entire being as focused intention. You become a bindu, a seed point, a point from which your life flowers as a manifestation of your soul, your spirit, your essence, your deep intention.

Attention, intention. Attention, intention.

When you enter into intention, you receive the blessing of Source that says:

You are never separate from me. You are always one with me. Remain aware of yourself as energy, as intention, as love, as manifestation of the Order, Balance, Harmony and Flow of Source.

•

After reading these words, contemplating, reflecting and meditating, if you choose, come to a close once again with the words: "May all beings be happy, peaceful and free of suffering." Remember, these words help you to shift from the experience of quiet contemplation to your busy everyday life. When you work with energy, it's important to pay attention to your transitions. We live in a universe of different frequencies, different vibrations, different energies. We are always shifting from one to the other. When doing energy work, or meditating, we are in a peaceful, universal frequency of Order, Balance, Harmony and Flow. In everyday life we are in constantly shifting, often conflicting, frequencies. To take time with transitions helps us to stay centered in the ground of Order, Balance, Harmony and Flow.

CHAPTER ELEVEN

SourcePoint and the Evolution of Human Consciousness

It is humanity's duty to reconnect and resonate with this deep code of nature, beautifying our world and our relationships with eurhythmic forms and golden standards of excellence. As nature does effortlessly, our duty is nothing less than to transmute our world, transforming it into the heavenly state of beauty and symbiotic peace that it was always intended to be.

— Scott Olsen, *The Golden Section*

IF WE STUDY systems theory, we learn that a complex system inevitably experiences disturbance. It has to change. It evolves. Disruption happens and it can never go back to what it was previously. You can't just patch things up and try to get it to function as it used to. The system experiences *discontinuity*. It has to adjust, reorganize, and find a different way of continuing.

We can see this in the journey of personal healing. Illness, trauma, pain and loss all bring us to that experience of discontinuity. We long to return to how things used to be, but deep inside we know that isn't going to happen. We will never be exactly as we were before. And yet, we find that as we open to and participate in the transformation our healing accelerates. As we connect to the information of the Blueprint and receive the messages of our original, undisturbed health, our disrupted system finds a renewed Order, Balance, Harmony and Flow, a new way of continuing. So really there is ultimately no break, no discontinuity. The disruption to the system becomes the ground for transformation and growth.

Connecting with the Blueprint does not return us to some immutable, perfect state of Order, Balance, Harmony and Flow. The information and energy of the Blueprint are always interacting with the disturbances and stresses we experience. Health is not some static state to be attained or returned to. It is movement, life and change: a dance of balance and imbalance, order and disorder, harmony and conflict, flow and fixation. Many systems theorists have said that life exists on the delicate balance between order and chaos. Too much order, the system becomes rigid; too little, and it disintegrates. Health is that delicate balance.

We can see this in our modern world. Humanity, the Earth, the atmosphere, the rain forests, the deserts, the oceans, rivers and lakes, animals, birds, and bugs—we are a complex system experiencing drastic disruption on a global scale. We are living in the midst of a profound discontinuity. Old ways aren't working, and the new has yet to fully emerge. What better time to connect with the fundamental information and energy of Order, Balance, Harmony and Flow, for the benefit of the whole system? Systems theory teaches us that if one part of a system is out of balance, the whole will be affected. *What we do to the web we do to ourselves.* That's why this chapter focuses on the evolution of *human* consciousness. It's why in SourcePoint Therapy we focus on the Blueprint for *human* health. If you look around, humans are the cause of the problem. Period. The Whole can survive without us. Whether it can survive with us is the question.

The Earth has consciousness. It is a sentient being. It feels what is done to it and it reacts. The vast information-energy-consciousness field of Source that gives rise to us as humans also gives rise to the stars, suns, planets and our very own Earth. The Earth has its Blueprint. The ordering forces are always at work to sustain the life of the Earth, to return it to Order, Balance, Harmony and Flow.

In our physical bodies, obstructions to the flow of healthy information from the Blueprint develop as a result of our accumulated experiences in incarnation. Imbalance and disorder manifest. When the body is out of balance it seeks to restore itself however it can, struggling with blockages and disconnection. The Earth is now a body out of balance. It has its own accumulated experience, which includes centuries of abuse. From this point of view tidal waves, earthquakes, volcanic eruptions, natural disasters and man-made ones, are not isolated phenomena. The energies of

Order, Balance, Harmony and Flow are always responding to obstructions, blockages, disorder, imbalance and conflict present in the Earth's field, attempting to restore Order.

The ordering forces will not tolerate the abuse the Earth continues to receive from us human beings. Just as the body has its guardian energies, so does the Earth. The guardian energies of the Earth are doing their work. The Earth will probably be around for millions of years to come. It has the power to heal itself. The cycle of life will continue, but the question is: will human beings choose to participate in that cycle of renewal, transformation, and rebirth that is the activity of the Blueprint? Or will we destroy ourselves and perhaps take all other life on Earth along with us?

What we come to understand when we align ourselves with the information of the Blueprint is obvious to those with eyes to see and ears to hear. It's nothing we all don't know already—except for those who don't seem to want to know it. The Earth itself is saying to human beings: *You have to STOP. You have to radically redefine what human life is about, or there will be no more life—as you have known it—on the earth.*

Stopping means taking time to pay attention to yourself and your relationship to the greater web of life. The intention of SourcePoint Therapy is to assist in bringing greater Order, Balance, Harmony and Flow to a world that is out of balance. As individuals strengthen their awareness of and connection to the Blueprint, then the greater Order, Balance, Harmony and Flow of the Earth's energy and of humanity's energy is brought into greater alignment. *What you do to the web you do to yourself. Yes, and what you do to yourself, you do to the web.*

The evolution of human consciousness demands the creation of a conscious self. This involves a shift in perspective on the self. From the SourcePoint perspective, the goal of the spiritual path is no longer to transcend or abandon the self, including the physical body, but to transform our experience of it, recognizing the physical body, individual consciousness and universal energy as one. We can come to experience the fundamental nature of the self as the Order, Balance, Harmony and Flow inherent in the universal energy. In this transformation a conscious self is born: one that delights in its existence, recognizes its interconnection with all being, and makes conscious choices that serve the Whole. Our aspiration then is to live in alignment and harmony with the greater Self of Order, Balance, Harmony and Flow. The conscious self recognizes its oneness with the natural order, while still taking responsibility for itself as an individual choice-making entity.

The choices you make influence not only your personal future evolution but also that of the collective human consciousness. Human consciousness is simply a composite. We are all a part of it: we all contribute to it. As people become aware of themselves as consciousness and energy, as we develop a heightened sensitivity to the subtle interactions of energy that underlie every event, then life here on earth begins to transform.

Empathy is a key factor in the ongoing evolution of human consciousness. When you feel another's experience, when you experience both yourself and the other *as energy* and see the subtle nuances of energy interacting with energy, it becomes more difficult to be domineering, aggressive and violent. Naturally, the tendency of the human to share, co-operate and communicate manifests more frequently. This is a huge step in the evolution of human consciousness.

The principles and practices of SourcePoint Therapy can help people become more sensitive to their own energies and those of others. When people understand the nature of energy they become more able to work with each other, to bring harmony and flow to their interactions. Instead of two rigidities both trying to impose their respective rigidity on the other, you have two different harmonies seeking to harmonize with each other. If you are interested in the evolution of human consciousness, it's your responsibility to look inward and examine yourself, your interactions, and your understanding of your fundamental nature.

The Blueprint contains the information of the highest potential for the human being. From the SourcePoint perspective we could say the full potential of the human being *is* health. And health in its highest sense for human beings means the ability to live together on earth in harmony with the Earth, all our relations, and the universal Order. Health means living in the spirit of community, cooperation and sharing.

We are at a point where the old view of evolution has to shift. We've been told our evolution depends on being constantly in survival mode. It's a model based on control, domination and aggression: *I'm going to survive by protecting myself and mine at all costs.* Now, in order to survive as a species, and allow the earth to find its natural balance, we as humans have to understand that our survival depends on cooperation, sharing, communication, and working together for the greater good. This is another huge shift. To accomplish this, once again we each have to take personal responsibility.

What does personal responsibility look like in these times? Many of us ask ourselves what we can possibly to do to help. Forces beyond our control are at work, and it's easy to feel quite helpless. Of course there are many actions we can take in the outer world that positively affect our environment in ways great and small. And, there's another approach, perhaps equally important. Here's a story that I have heard many times and encountered in many sources. It gives us an idea of what personal responsibility in a time of disorder might involve.

This story was originally told by Richard Wilhelm, Sinologist, to his good friend Carl Jung, and purports to relate events Wilhelm actually witnessed. Apparently there was a village in China that had been experiencing severe drought for many years. The villagers had tried everything they knew how to do in the way of ritual and appealing to the gods, but nothing worked. In desperation, they asked a rainmaker from a distant province to help them. When the rainmaker arrived, he did nothing. He simply requested to retire to a simple hut and not be disturbed. He remained there for three days, and at the end of that time it began to rain. When the rainmaker emerged, he explained that he did nothing to make the rain come. Upon arriving in the village he had experienced that the village was not in the Tao. The natural order was not operating. Because of this state of disorder, he also was disturbed and not in harmony. Therefore he retired to bring himself into the Tao, and then naturally the rain came.

The resonance here with SourcePoint is this: the Tao can be described as the fundamental Order, Balance, Harmony and Flow of the universal energy. It's another word for Source. In his own way, the rainmaker simply aligned himself with that fundamental Order, Balance, Harmony and Flow. He connected to the Blueprint.

And the rain fell.

This story tells us what to do in this state of discontinuity, disorder and transformation that we are living through, that our world is experiencing. We don't have to retire to a hut. We do have to find ways to live in alignment with the fundamental cosmic Order. In doing so, we help our Earth and all beings that dwell upon it. We nourish the vision of a humanity living together in alignment, in harmony, in health.

All of this can sound like an impossible ideal. And yet, for any vision to come into being, it must first be spoken. Then, it is important to continue to hold the vision, to focus on the possibility of transformation, to actualize it in every way possible. It's not a matter of blind faith, of believing that against all odds there will be such a paradise on earth. No one can promise it will happen—but if we persist in thinking that human beings are by nature greedy, aggressive and violent, if we continue to believe that the story of how it has been is how it has to be, then that's probably the story that perpetuates itself. However, if we hold the vision we're giving words to here, then that specific information is present in the human consciousness. We are cultivating seeds of Order, Balance, Harmony and Flow.

In SourcePoint what we are really working for, what we are really doing, is this: we give our full attention to the person before us, to the one who arrives in need of help, and thus we begin to actualize together our full human potential as human beings. As we also give full attention to our own actions and thoughts, to our relationships, to our way of being in the world, our alignment with the fundamental Order, Balance, Harmony, and Flow, we begin to actualize our full human potential. We evolve. We become healthy in every sense of the word.

Each person who practices SourcePoint for the benefit of another, who uses the methods for self-help, who explores the principles as a means of spiritual growth, is working to actualize his or her full human potential. If we hold the vision in our heart of all people experiencing their full human potential, of a world where people can live in harmony with each other, with the environment and with the greater Order, we assist the evolution of human consciousness.

We call this *far vision*. This isn't going to happen in our lifetimes. And yet the potential is there. We are not suggesting SourcePoint is going to save the world. It is one small way to help bring that information of Order, Balance, Harmony and Flow into this plane of existence, to actualize it in the human life. This is how we can contribute to the evolution of human consciousness.

May all beings be happy, peaceful, and free of suffering!

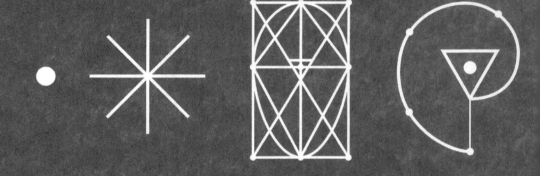

CHAPTER 12

The Story of SourcePoint

After you know my poems are not poems, then we can begin to discuss poetry.

—Ryokan, translated by John Stevens, *One Robe, One Bowl*

PERHAPS YOU REMEMBER the quote from Ellsworth Kelley at the beginning of Chapter Seven: "The work itself is what's important." That's why we've left our personal story of SourcePoint Therapy until the end. SourcePoint is not about us. It's not our story. It's information that's come to us, and it's our task to receive it, work with it, refine it and disseminate it. It's a gift that's been given us, and we share that gift with you. If what has been said resonates for you, opens some doors, is helpful in some way, that's what matters. Continue to explore and open, investigate and practice. What matters is transformation. What matters is your path in this world and what helps you along it. Our story is not what matters. At the same time, the fact is, it's one of the things that we do as human beings: we share our stories. Life happens, stars move in their cycles, seasons change—and we tell the stories. As humans, we want to know where things come from, how they came to be. We love to know the stories of origin.

When people ask, "Where does SourcePoint Therapy come from?" our answer is simple. It comes from the Blueprint itself. Where else could it come from? In many indigenous cultures, shamans work with native herbs as medicine. When these healers are asked how they know which plants are appropriate for different people, the reply is often: "The plants tell us." So it is when people ask us how we discovered where the points are located and what they do. We too can only say, "The points told us."

Our story begins, then, as so many do. Once upon a time, there was a point, in time, in space, beyond time and space, in consciousness, in energy, in memory and beyond memory—there was a point. And from this single point, it all emerged...

One day in 1995, Bob and I sat down together with the intention of doing an Awareness session in relation to his Rolfing® work. What's an Awareness session? It's the work I've personally done with people for years, long before SourcePoint. In these sessions I access light, energy and information for the benefit of others. I am in touch with and speaking from an information-energy field I simply call the Awareness. This Awareness sees more deeply, widely and with greater perception than is possible for me in my ordinary consciousness. People might describe this as channeling, but as the process has evolved, I have come to see it differently. A spirit being does not enter into me as channels say when they describe their work; rather, I enter into a greater Awareness, a consciousness beyond my ordinary one, yet not separate from it.

In this particular session on this particular day, Bob wanted to explore what could be done to help a client who wasn't getting better. This person would experience some improvement, but it wouldn't hold. Anyone who does any kind of therapeutic work or who has gone through a healing process knows this is not an uncommon situation. We wanted to explore in Awareness what could be done to help the work hold better.

Beginning that day, through this process of entering into a greater Awareness, the points revealed themselves and told us what they were for. To some, this may make our approach seem unscientific, esoteric, and difficult to prove. From a modern, Western, rational mindset this would be so. However, human culture has a long history of receiving guidance either directly from Source, or from intermediaries. In the past, channeling has been equated with possession by a spirit or entity. Oracles go into trances. Mediums contact the dead. Shamans journey to other realms or dimensions. While all of these are time-honored traditions and ways of accessing information from a greater consciousness, to acknowledge this path as a source of information in today's world can be to invite scorn, derision and dismissal.

Perhaps in the 21st century, in light of what we know of the quantum universe, we need to reconsider this attitude. First, we could redefine what is commonly called channeling. Perhaps such a process is simply accessing the all-encompassing energy-information field in which we dwell. We know so little, really, about consciousness, the brain, the body and the universe. We discover more every day. Perhaps we are so intimately connected to the meta-energy-information field that if we just tune in we can receive all kinds of information. Could intuition simply be attunement to that field? As scientists explore the brain, body, and universe, we may each come to know ourselves as channels, open to the greater consciousness, able to connect with and enter into that universal energy-information field and access the information stored there.

So, together, through what we call Awareness sessions, Bob and I found the principles and practices of SourcePoint. The first point revealed itself in that session in 1995. It was the Source Point, on the right side of the body. The information came slowly, with these words: *There is a point, located, yes, on the right side of the body... in the region of the navel ... but further out from the body. At the level of the navel...*

I often lie down when I do these sessions, and as this information began to emerge Bob held this point for me. We clarified the location. We were originally told only that this point could strengthen the vital life force and, in answer to our specific question, that perhaps it could help work to hold longer. Bob began to explore the use of this point, and found it did indeed seem to support the work he was doing. Then, slowly, through further Awareness sessions and in response to our specific questions, the other points revealed themselves, along with more information about their function and purpose. What was to become "SourcePoint Therapy," as we finally named it in 2004, had begun to emerge.

All of the information that came to us in this way was tested, refined and developed in Bob's private practice. This practical application of the information is the foundation of what we teach. In addition, when we began to research further we discovered that the concepts and principles of SourcePoint had resonances in many traditions and healing modalities. As well, the writings of many contemporary physicists seemed to relate to what we were saying about an information field. This research helped us to formulate and articulate more clearly the information that was emerging.

Only when it began to appear that things were happening—results were occurring and people were experiencing benefits from these points and from the Blueprint—only then was the process given a name. Only after this, ten years from the time the information was first accessed, did we really begin sharing it with others. From the outset, we did this with the understanding that SourcePoint Therapy is an approach to working with energy that is meant to enhance whatever else people are doing for their health, whatever modality a practitioner is already using, whatever treatments a person is receiving at the physical level. As we shared the work others began to experience its positive benefits in their therapeutic work and their personal lives.

SourcePoint is an integration of all of our experiences in the thirty years or so preceding the time it began to emerge. We didn't set out to develop a method of energy work. Rather, it was a gift from Source. It arose from the Blueprint, the field of Order, Balance, Harmony and Flow of which we speak. It's been a delight and a wonder to watch it grow, take form and travel out into the world, where it continues to evolve and change. Our personal stories are one aspect of the story of SourcePoint, and we'd like to share a little of those here, to provide a background and context.

BOB'S STORY

I am sitting here in my painting studio looking at a painting I did this past winter, one of a series honoring the line. In sacred geometry, the line emerges from the singularity of the point to give birth to form. The line is the central organizing principle of Rolfing, the body itself, and my life. Copies of Wassily Kandinsky's *Point to Line to Plane* and *Concerning the Spiritual in Art*, written at the Bauhaus in 1924, sit on my desk next to books on functional morphology and embryology. Science, art, and spirituality are three threads in my life that have woven themselves together in the emergence of SourcePoint.

My interest in art developed early, and as I explored the arts I encountered this statement: *Architecture is the Mother of the Arts*. This led me to undertake professional training in architecture when I entered university. Architecture school demanded a thorough and disciplined study of the sciences as well as grounding in art and design; it spoke to the wide variety of interests that I held at the time and still do. After the conclusion of my architecture training I pursued a Master of Fine Arts both in London and at the Art Institute in Chicago. While in London I would spend my Saturday afternoons visiting the British museum and also a small bookstore nearby, which turned out to be an Anthroposophy center. I spent time reading Rudolph Steiner and studying Goethe's theories of color and the Ur phenomena.

I was also drawn, in 1966, to the work of the German artist Joseph Beuys, who has had an important influence on the development of modern art. His vision of the artist as shaman, healer and visionary touched something deep in my soul. Joseph Beuys and Rudolph Steiner both shared a profound interest in how form emerged from what Steiner termed "the etheric formative forces." [35] Many of Beuys' pieces directly referenced blackboard drawings and lectures from Rudolph Steiner. I was beginning to awaken not only to the commonality of science and art but also to see that healing arises from a unified field of human consciousness, which has its expression in the figure of the shaman.

Then, suddenly, the Vietnam War tore me out of Chicago and my studies and dropped me into an unexpected life as a conscientious objector in Toronto. There I met a group of others in the same position, who had all been associated with the Whole Earth Catalogue, an American counter-culture publication issued regularly from 1968-1972, and periodically thereafter. Together, we decided to start a Canadian version with each issue focusing on a different topic. I was asked to be the editor for an issue on healing. While doing research for that project I encountered the work of Dr. Ida Rolf, and was immediately interested. At the time she was teaching at Esalen, but I was not able to return to the United States to study with her. I did, however, begin to interview and study with a number of chiropractors, naturopaths, and osteopaths in Ontario. I soon encountered many emerging paradigms and the entire field of energy medicine. This included homeopathy, flower remedies and radionics, a method of energy work using energy frequencies. I was drawn to the further study of these methods.

In the midst of these pursuits, my own life took another unexpected turn, and at that point I was able to return to the United States to follow this new direction. I began my formal practice and study of Zen, which became the central organizing factor in my life for the next fifteen years. There was the line again, in the form of the kyosaku, the encouragement stick, the straight and narrow way. Simplicity. Zazen. That is another story, but, in relation to my later work and the development of SourcePoint, there was a core teaching of Zen that helped to shape all my future work: *all beings are whole and complete, lacking nothing.*

This teaching led me naturally to approach healing from the perspective of our essential wellness. Above all, my years in Zen instilled in me an appreciation of simplicity and directness, which I had sometimes found missing in the more esoteric approaches to energy healing I had encountered.

Over the last forty years, I have continued my studies in energy medicine, sacred geometry, consciousness, and shamanic healing, as well as Rolfing® and Biodynamic Craniosacral Therapy, and all of these, as well as SourcePoint Therapy, inform my work still. [36]

DONNA'S STORY

Any story has to choose its moment to begin, and when I think of where my story with SourcePoint begins, it goes all the way back to childhood. As a child, I used to experience frequently what I called my "moments of perfect happiness." These experiences would come upon me suddenly, for no reason, seldom when anything special was occurring, at random as far as I could tell. I couldn't make them happen. They were characterized by a sudden shift in the air, as though everything came suddenly into focus, was bright and clear and soft all at the same time. These moments were invariably accompanied by a feeling of wholeness and completeness, although I did not use those words then. Everything was right, just as it was, in harmony with everything else, at peace. It was as though the whole universe shimmered with happiness. For a moment, I would feel absolutely, utterly content.

Later in my life I described this experience as the Presence of Awareness. It's what I feel when I am engaged in my Awareness sessions. There was a long gap in my adolescent years and my twenties when I didn't experience this often. Then, what I call simply the Awareness returned to me in my late thirties, just after I left the Zen Center that had been the focus of my life for the preceding fifteen years.

During these years at the Zen Center I experienced grounding, structure and discipline that allowed me to open up to new energies and experiences in consciousness through regular daily meditation as well as intensive retreats. I am forever grateful for that grounding.

Bob and I met at the Zen Center and married there. We eventually left that community in 1985. I had been on the staff of the Center for many years, as had Bob, and he had been teaching for some years also when we left. And then, suddenly, there we were, out in the world again, with a teenage son and a need to support ourselves. For a while, Bob did construction work and I was a secretary. It turned out that the woman I was replacing at my new job was a trance medium. I actually had little idea of what that was, but I was fascinated. Feeling in need of some guidance, I went to see her.

In the midst of my first reading with her something inside me just said *yes* and began to open up. Looking back, it feels as though something I had been waiting for began to happen. I couldn't put it into words, but the experience of receiving guidance from beyond was intimately familiar. I knew the process; my whole body-mind-spirit resonated with it. I loved the thought of being a channel but I wasn't thinking about channeling spirits. Rather I realized that's what we all are, really. We're just channels through which the cosmic energy manifests itself. The more my sense of "I" gets out of the way, the clearer the channel is. I began to pray to be a clear channel for love and light to enter the world. I never expected my prayer to be answered so literally.

One summer night in 1986 I sat down with my journal to write, as I usually did. But this night, as I began, there was that shift in the air I knew so well from childhood. I found myself surrounded by a light, bright, and clear Presence. My handwriting shifted dramatically; it was no longer obviously mine. I watched my hand move across the page without knowing what I was writing. When the writing stopped, I discovered I had received helpful messages that applied to the continuing transition I was experiencing in my life. This went on for six months, every time I wrote in my journal. For those six months, I have no record of my personal life or feelings, just the Awareness. And now, the handwriting covering those pages is completely illegible to me. At the time I could read it easily, but not now.

During this period, I continued to work with the trance medium, I meditated a lot, and I wrote a lot. Simultaneously, I returned to university to get my Masters Degree in Social Work. After six months of writing, it felt like time to see what would happen if I sat down with my journal to write, but then began to speak instead of write. Would the information still come through? Was I meant to speak words of guidance aloud? Bob was with me when I did this. Instantly, the Awareness was there, saying: *Yes, yes, yes.* Sessions still begin that way, with deep affirmation of all that is.

Fast forwarding, after graduating with my MSW and working for a time as a family therapist and high school guidance counselor, I spent the next twenty years or so doing Awareness Sessions with people, on a group and individual basis, in the U.S and Europe, in person, and by phone. Through this work, the Awareness touched hundreds of people with its guidance, insight and light. During this period I experienced how the greater Awareness reflects each person with care and attention, responding to each one as a completely unique being, without judgment, with infinite patience. I learned so much about energy and consciousness and life in this material world. With the Awareness I worked with energy long before SourcePoint began to emerge, and much of the material in my book, *The Vibrant Life: Simple Meditations to Use Your Energy Effectively* (Sentient Publications 2006) came from this period. In these years I also encountered many teachers in many spiritual traditions who enriched my life and practice. During this time, I believe deep intention was at work, preparing me for the emergence of SourcePoint.

In 1993 I had a dream, and all I brought back from this dream when I awoke was the single phrase: *The basic pattern of life is a diamond*. I was intrigued by this, but had no idea what it meant. Nothing further came and I let it go. And then one day, a couple of years later, the first point made itself known in an Awareness session and my story merged into the story of SourcePoint. Working with Bob on developing this approach to energy work, for many years now, has immeasurably deepened and enhanced my experience of the Presence of Awareness. I feel blessed every day by the gifts that have come through that Presence. My life has been an adventure in the exploration of consciousness and energy, and it makes me immeasurably happy that those explorations can now be of benefit to others.

As SourcePoint continues to develop, its story grows and changes too. Everyone who studies it, practices it, or receives it, becomes a part of the story. SourcePoint becomes a part of you. I hope it opens doors into new dimensions for you as it has for me. May it bring you a new vision of who you are, and a more profound connection to the beauty and wonder of all that is.

Poems, perhaps, give us hints of stories that are beyond words. The story of SourcePoint as told in this book comes to completion for now, as it began, with a poem. This one came to me one day during a SourcePoint Module One.

I am (you are)
tree and star
ocean and wave
moon and tide
mermaid and angel
earth and air and fire and water
brilliant dark radiating space
a dance of pattern
a wondrous construction
the breathing idea
of an impossible Mind
emerging
into
possibility

May all beings be happy, peaceful and free of suffering!

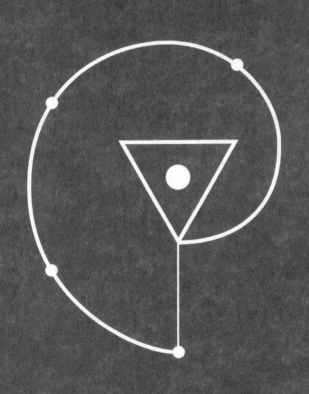

SOURCEPOINT THERAPY® TRAINING

AS THE STORY of SourcePoint continues, we invite you to join the Source-Point community and expand your exploration through participating in our ongoing trainings. I once attended a healing ceremony with an African healer. I have always remembered what he said: in his country healing is a community affair. Healing does not happen in isolation, in a small room, for one hour, with one other person. The ceremony I attended went on for two days, in community.

It is in this spirit we conduct our trainings. We are committed to exploring this field of energy and consciousness and healing with people in an intimate, relaxed and supportive environment, providing depth and individual attention. When we come together in community with the intention of transformation, learning, growing and sharing, we enter a supportive energy field that intensifies by the hour. We experience this regularly in our workshops. As we talk about the Blueprint, as we connect to the Source, as we learn the practices and share our experiences, the field is palpable, tangible and powerful.

Our intention with SourcePoint Therapy is not merely to teach yet another approach to energy work, it is also to offer support, community, guidance and sustenance for healthcare practitioners of all kinds, as well as those who are working on their own healing and personal growth. Each workshop provides the opportunity to share, to listen, to go deep with others into the wondrous, clear energy field we call the Blueprint, and to continue your own process of self-healing.

The path of energy work involves a lot of personal transformation. It's not just a collection of techniques. It's not a quick zap. It's a path into and through the unknown, the possible, the dream. It requires a commitment to exploring a world beyond the ordinary, beyond the limits of your current thinking. In teaching SourcePoint we provide individual attention and the opportunity to go deep; we are committed to guiding you along your way in that world, providing the benefit of our experience and understanding, in the hope that what we call SourcePoint Therapy can bring greater Order, Balance, Harmony and Flow to individuals and the world.

The original intention of SourcePoint is to provide an energetic foundation and support for healthcare practitioners seeking to explore the dimension of energy in their work. It does not take the place of medical care for physical or psychological conditions, but we believe it can support such work. Practitioners of all kinds have found this to be true: Structural Integrators, Massage Therapists, Physical Therapists, Acupuncturists, Nurses, Medical Doctors, Psychotherapists, Nutritionists, and Energy Workers with different backgrounds. Yoga teachers find it supports their understanding of Yoga and that working with the Blueprint enhances their teaching.

However, no prior experience in bodywork or health care is necessary if one wants to explore the practices and principles for oneself. Many people come to our trainings saying they have just always wanted to know more about working with energy. SourcePoint is a good foundation for that exploration.

Basic SourcePoint Therapy training consists of three modules. The modules are as follows:

MODULE ONE:

THE BLUEPRINT: FUNDAMENTAL PRINCIPLES AND PRACTICES OF SOURCEPOINT THERAPY®

This module introduces the theory of the Blueprint of health, teaches energy scanning techniques for locating blockages in the physical body that are obstructing the flow of information from the Blueprint, and instructs the student in the principles and use of the Ten Essential Points: the Diamond Points, Golden Rectangle Points, the Sacral Point and the Navel Point.

MODULE TWO:

THE INNER TEMPLE: THE SACRUM, THE GUARDIANS OF THE BODY AND ENERGETIC STRUCTURES.

This module focuses on points that open, relax, and balance the sacrum, as well as specific holds to support the sacrum. We learn and practice the Guardian Points that activate the natural guardian energies of the body. Participants work with energetic structures in the energy field to bring balance and order to the flow of energy in the physical body: The Golden Line (the midline), the Stick Figure, the Gold Point, the Crescent Moon and the Eight-Pointed Star. The SourcePoint approach to the chakras is also covered in this module.

MODULE THREE:

ADVANCED PRINCIPLES AND PRACTICES: WORKING WITH TRAUMA, KARMA AND EMOTION; DRAWING OUT EXTERNAL INVASIVE ENERGIES FROM THE BODY

Explores advanced use of the Navel Point for addressing blockages at the levels of trauma, karma and emotion. In-depth work with the Guardians of the body; drawing out external invasive energies from the physical body; further practice with the Stick Figure as an energetic foundation for trauma work. Includes complete review and refinement of material from the previous modules, advanced practicum and work with integration of other modalities.

These modules must be taken in sequence beginning with Module One. The first two modules are each three days long, and the third module is a six-day training, in two three-day segments. At the end of the first module you can begin integrating SourcePoint Therapy® into your practice of therapeutic work if you are a professional healthcare practitioner, or continue to explore for yourself if your interest is more personal. At the end of Module Three you receive a Certificate of Completion stating only that you have completed the basic SourcePoint Therapy® training. After Module Three we offer Advanced Intensives and mentorships that no longer proceed in sequential progression but give people the opportunity to go deeper into the work, refine their understanding and practice and continue their personal healing journey.

Please see our website www.sourcepointtherapy.com for ongoing updates on workshop dates and locations.

CONTACT INFORMATION

Further information is available on our website. Guided audio meditations that relate specifically to the meditations and practices in this book can be found on our blog, which can be accessed from the website. On the website you will also find brief video presentations, a gallery of Bob Schrei's SourcePoint artwork, training schedules, and contact information.

www.sourcepointtherapy.com

ABOUT THE AUTHORS

BOB SCHREI is a Certified Advanced Rolfer in practice since 1986, a licensed massage therapist and biodynamic cranial-sacral therapist, an artist and former Zen teacher, and the co-founder of SourcePoint Therapy® with his wife and partner in energy work, Donna Thomson.

DONNA THOMSON is an intuitive, meditation guide, MSW, and author of the book *Simple Meditations to Use your Energy Effectively* (Sentient Publications 2006). They live and practice in Santa Fe, New Mexico, and teach SourcePoint Therapy® in many U.S locations as well as internationally.

photo by Josh Schrei

ACKNOWLEDGEMENTS

We wish first to acknowledge the many spiritual teachers and traditions of the healing arts that have informed our explorations and studies in consciousness, energy, spirit and healing.

We also want to express our deep gratitude to all those in the United States, Europe, Japan and Brazil who have supported SourcePoint Therapy® with their commitment to its study and practice, and especially to those in many locations who have organized workshops and helped us to share this work. So many wonderful people in so many places have played a role in the story of SourcePoint.

We would like to acknowledge especially the contribution of Ray McCall, Certified Advanced Rolfer and Advanced Faculty Member at the Rolf Institute® of Structural Integration in Boulder, Colorado. From the early days of SourcePoint he has helped it to take root and grow. We deeply appreciate his support.

Thanks to Richard Wehrman and Merlinwood Books for the book design and publishing, and to Dave Sheldon, Elizabeth Sullivan, Eva Rose Goetz and Andrea Clusen for their reading and suggestions. Elizabeth in particular patiently read the book on every one of its versions; many thanks to her. Special gratitude goes to Satara Bixby for her editing, proofreading and careful attention to details. And more special thanks to JoAnne O'Brien-Levin (writetowisdom.com) for helping me bring the book to fruition at last.

REFERENCES

CHAPTER 1

1. Albert Einstein, *Cosmic Religion: With Other Opinions and Aphorisms* (New York: Covici-Friede, 1931), 97.

2. Lynne McTaggart, *The Field: The Quest for the Secret Force of the Universe* (New York: Quill, 2002), xiii.

3. Ray McCall, private conversation with author, August 2012.

4. "matrix," *TheFreeDictionary.com*, 2013. http://www.thefreedictionary.com/matrix (accessed 25 November 2013)

5. Candace B. Pert, PhD, *Molecules of Emotion: The Science Behind Mind-Body Medicine* (New York: Scribner, 1997), 257.

6. Richard Tarnas, *The Passion of the Western Mind: Understanding the Ideas that have Shaped Our World View* (New York: Ballantine Books, 1991), 10.

7. See: Carl Jung, *Archetypes and the Collective Unconscious: Collected Works of C.G. Jung Volume 9 Part 1* (Princeton, New Jersey: Princeton University Press, 1981).

8. Laurens van der Post, *Jung and the Story of Our Time* (New York: Vintage Books, 1977), 217.

9. Dr. Yeshi Donden, *Healing from the Source: The Science and Lore of Tibetan Medicine* (Ithaca, New York: Snow Lion Publications, 2000), 21.

10. Neil Gumenick, "The Spirits of the Points: The Liver Meridian - Part I," *Acupuncture Today*, February, 2012, Volume 13, Issue 02, accessed June 14, 2015, http://www.acupuncturetoday.com/mpacms/at/article. php?id=32527.

11. Ida Rolf, *The Integration of Human Structures* (New York: Harper and Row, 1971), 1.

12. Michael Kern, *Wisdom in the Body* (Berkeley, California: North Atlantic Books, 2005), 33.

13. Rupert Sheldrake, *Morphic Resonance and Morphic Fields: An Introduction*, February 2005, accessed June 14, 2015, http://www.sheldrake. org/Articles&Papers/papers/morphic/morphic_intro.html.

14. *Of Sound Mind and Body: Music & Vibrational Healing*, Interview with Rupert Sheldrake, MACROmedia Publishing, 2010. Film program, accessed June 14, 2015, http://www.cymaticsource.com/cymaticsdvd. html

15. Roger Penrose, Stuart Hameroff, Henry P. Stapp and Deepak Chopra, *Consciousness in the Universe: Quantum Physics, Evolution, Brain and Mind*, (Cambridge, MA: Cosmology Science Publishers, 2011), 933.

16. F. David Peat, *Synchronicity: The Bridge Between Matter and Mind*, (New York: Bantam Books, 1987), 94.

17. Ervin Laszlo, *Science and the Akashic Field: An Integral Theory of Everything*, (Rochester, Vermont: Inner Traditions, 2004), 141.

CHAPTER 2

18. Sandra Blakeslee and Matthew Blakeslee, *The Body Has a Mind of Its Own: How Body Maps in Your Brain Help You Do (Almost) Everything Better*, (New York: Random House, 2008), 5.

19. Lynne McTaggart, *The Intention Experiment*, (New York: Free Press, 2007), 151ff.

20. Scott Suvow, "The History of Acupuncture," accessed June 14, 2015, https://www.acufinder.com/Acupuncture+Information/Detail/The+History+of+Acupuncture.

21. Lama Nyoshul Khenpo Jamyang Dorje, "The Mirror of Essential Points," accessed June 14, 2015, http://www.nyingma.com/artman/publish/mirror_dzogchen.shtml

CHAPTER 3

22. Michael S. Schneider, *A Beginner's Guide to Constructing the Universe: the Mathematical Archetypes of Nature, Art and Science*, (New York: Harper, 1995), xx.

23. A. Garret Lisi and James Owen Weatherall, "The Geometric Theory of Everything," *Scientific American* (December 2010), 55.

24. Ibid. 54.

25. Robert Lawlor, *Sacred Geometry, Philosophy and Practice* (London: Thames and Hudson, 1982), 4.

26. M. Eliade, *Myth and Reality*, (New York: Harper and Row, 1968), 25.

CHAPTER 4

27. Brian Stross, "The Mesoamerican Sacrum Bone: Dcorway to the Otherworld," accessed June 14, 2015, http://research.famsi.org/aztlan/uploads/papers/stross-sacrum.pdf, 38.

28. *Oxford English Dictionary*, s. v. "sacrum."

CHAPTER 5

29. See Herbert Benson, MD, *Timeless Healing: The Power and Biology of Belief*, (New York: Scribner, 1997).

30. Candace B. Pert, PhD, *Molecules of Emotion: The Science Behind Mind Body Medicine* (New York: Scribner, 1997), 185.

31. Fritjof Capra, *The Web of Life: A New Scientific Understanding of Living Systems,* (New York: Anchor Books, 1996), 279.

CHAPTER 6

32. Bruce Lipton, *Biology of Belief,* (Santa Rosa, California: Mountain of Love/Elite Books, 2005), 120.

CHAPTER 7

33. See Malidoma Somé, *Of Water and the Spirit,* (New York: Penguin Group, 1994).

CHAPTER 9

34. Kusala Bhikshu, "Was the Tsunami Caused by Karma? - A Buddhist View," accessed June 14, 2015, http://www.urbandharma.org/udharma9/karma.html.

CHAPTER 12

35. See Rudolf Steiner, *The Etheric Formative Forces in Cosmos, Earth and Man; A Path of Investigation Into the World of the Living, Volume 1,* (New York: Anthroposophic Press, 1932).

36. Bob's Story. This material originally appeared in an article by Bob Schrei and Ray McCall in the *International Association for Structural Integration Yearbook 2010,* March 2010.